I0819907

The *Alexandreis* of Walter of Châtillon

THE MIDDLE AGES SERIES

A complete list of books in the series
is available from the publisher.

The *Alexandreis* of Walter of Châtillon

A Twelfth-Century Epic

A verse translation by
David Townsend

PENN

University of Pennsylvania Press

Philadelphia

10 9 8 7 6 5 4 3 2 1

Published by
University of Pennsylvania Press
Philadelphia, Pennsylvania 19104

Library of Congress Cataloging-in-Publication Data
Walter, of Châtillon, fl. 1170-1180.
[Alexandreis. English]
The Alexandreis of Walter of Châtillon : a twelfth-century epic :
a verse translation / by David Townsend.
p. cm. — (University of Pennsylvania Press Middle Ages series)
Includes bibliographical references (p.) and index.
ISBN 0-8122-3347-6 (cloth : alk. paper)
1. Alexander, the Great, 356-323 B.C.—Romances. 2. Epic poetry,
Latin (Medieval and modern)—Translations into English.
I. Townsend, David. II. Title. III. Series: Middle Ages series.
PA8310.G3A713 1997
873'.03—dc20 96-27676
CIP

For Talestris, Queen of the Amazons;
for the Scythian messenger;
para los Zapatistas:
the heroes in the margins of the Text

Contents

Acknowledgments

My debts of gratitude are many and various: to George Rigg, most collegial of colleagues, for sustained enthusiasm and support; to Claire Fanger, an accomplished translator and a keen critic; to Lois Kuznets, for ideas exchanged over the years, mostly in the kitchen; to Catherine Conybeare, Carla DeSantis, and Rob Moody, medieval Latinists with whom I shared readings of Walter that significantly shaped my understanding of his work; and especially to Maura Lafferty, who made suggestions for the notes. In 1992–93, Arianne Kossack, May Sham, and Adam Smears participated in a University of Toronto mentorship program for exceptional high school students; they helped me identify those passages for which the general reader might require elucidation in the notes, and to sketch out the kinds of annotation they considered helpful. The University of Toronto Office of Research Services provided me with research funds in 1990 that allowed me to spend time with manuscripts of the *Alexandreis* housed in British libraries: exposure to material evidence of the codices afforded insights into medieval receptions of the poem that otherwise would have occurred to me, if at all, only later and less vividly. To my partner Rob Norquay I owe thanks for his support and patience at times when the project encroached on our lives. Finally, my most profound gratitude goes to Scott Westrem, whose erudition is matched only by his generosity, and whose meticulous comments made the translation both more accurate and more graceful than it would otherwise have been, although many flaws remain despite his good offices.

Introduction

The Poem and Its Author

Walter of Châtillon's ten-book epic on the life of Alexander the Great is one of the high achievements of twelfth-century literature. It ranks among the finest works of Latin literature in a century that also produced Bernard Silvestris, Nigel of Canterbury, the *Ysengrimus* poet, Alan of Lille, Walter Map, and Joseph of Exeter. In artistry and intelligence it loses nothing by comparison to the first flowerings of European vernacular literature. Yet Walter's work, while today better known and more widely read than it was before the appearance of Marvin Colker's critical edition in 1978,[1] remains largely an object of specialist scrutiny. Most undergraduate students and committed amateurs of medieval literature have never read it. Scholars of vernacular literature, with some notable exceptions, refer to it more or less cursorily as a work of ancillary interest.

But to Walter's own generation and the centuries following the poem's composition, it was a work of undisputed preeminence. Over two hundred manuscripts survive, the majority of them dating from the thirteenth century, but significant numbers representing the fourteenth and fifteenth centuries as well.[2] The poem was printed in 1487 (Rouen), and again three times in the sixteenth century, in 1513 (Strasbourg), 1541 (Ingolstadt), and 1558 (Lyons). Few works of medieval literature survive in such a copious transmission: the *Roman de la Rose* and Dante's *Divine Comedy* survive in roughly comparable numbers of manuscripts, while Chaucer's *Canterbury Tales* are extant in fewer than one hundred. Literary quality, and even influence, are of course not to be so easily measured as this; but Walter's poem certainly loomed as large in the literary milieux of Jean de Meun, Boccaccio, Dante, Chaucer, and Gower as do works by Chaucer, Milton,

1. Marvin Colker, ed., *Galteri de castellione Alexandreis* (Padua: Antenore, 1978).
2. Colker provides a census of manuscripts on pp. xxxiii–xxxviii of his edition.

and Tennyson in ours. Its disappearance from the canon after a sustained popularity might suggest instead an analogy to *Orlando Furioso*. Nor was Walter's poem simply copied and read widely: it was studied intensively as a standard text of the literary curriculum, as a plethora of glosses in many surviving manuscripts attests.[3]

If the poem's interest were only historical in nature—if it were only a curious monument to the otherness of tastes which modern readers cannot share—its neglect today might be allowed to go on without intervention. But the *Alexandreis* is also a work of qualities that shifts in literary expectation have not rendered inaccessible. Readers today can still find in the poem, and often find easily and intuitively, an extraordinary subtlety, a keen intelligence, a beauty in turns lyrical and outlandish, and at times even an uncanny postmodernity. It rewards the reader as richly as do many of the better-known texts we think of as the heart of medieval European literature. It deserves to be read alongside the medieval authors we have come to see as canonical, and to be read, by those for whom the original Latin is inaccessible, in a translation that tries to allow the reader an experience of the work as poetry.

We know less than we might wish of the poem's author and of the circumstances of its composition. Walter was probably born around 1135. A number of biographical notices survive in the *accessus* (introductions) included among the glosses of some manuscripts.[4] The details of these sketches are mutually contradictory. Walter seems to have been born in Lille. After studies in Paris and Reims, and after directing the school of Laon, he headed a school at one of the several towns of Châtillon in northeastern France—Châtillon-sur-Marne is the prime candidate. It is by his association with Châtillon that he is usually known. There he composed *quedam ludicra*, "light verses," which presumably encompass the love lyrics and moral satires in accentual meters for which we count him among the chief practitioners of the so-called Goliardic style.[5] Subsequent to a realization that the liberal arts don't pay, he may have gone on to study law in Bologna. Thereafter he entered into the service of Guillaume des Blanches

3. On the glosses to the poem, see Marvin Colker, "Note on the History of the Commentary on the Alexandreis," *Medium Aevum* 28 (1959), 97–98, and R. DeCesare, *Glosse latine e antico-francese all' "Alexandreis" di Gautier de Châtillon* (Milan: Vita e Pensiero, 1951).

4. For the biographical details that follow, see the Latin glosses printed by Colker in the introduction and on p. 494 of his edition.

5. These texts are edited by Karl Strecker, *Die Lieder Walters von Châtillon in der Handschrift 351 von St. Omer* (Berlin: Weidmann, 1925) and *Moralisch-satirische Gedichte Walters von Châtillon* (Heidelberg: Carl Winter, 1929).

Mains (William of the White Hands), brother-in-law of Louis VII, uncle of Philip Augustus, archbishop of Sens and subsequently of Reims.[6] The *Alexandreis* is dedicated to William, as the opening of Book One and the close of Books Five and Ten attest. The initial letters of the poem's ten books spell out GUILLERMUS. One thirteenth-century biographical gloss from Paris, Bibliothèque nationale, MS lat. 8358, fol. 91v suggests that Walter composed the poem to regain William's favor. According to the anecdote, Walter was jealous of William's sexual liaison with a cleric named Berterus; he took his revenge by contriving the recitation of a scurrilous jingle at the papal curia, thus effectively "outing" the archbishop (and himself) before the Pope:

Some say that the work's instigation lay in the restoration of Master Walter's love in the sight of Lord William Archbishop of Reims, and in the enmity which he had incurred in his sight because of Master Berterus. If the truth is fit to speak, the Lord Archbishop William was using Berterus sexually, and Master Walter envied him. And indeed, at one point it happened that the archbishop sent Master Berterus to Rome to plead his case. Master Walter, thinking that he might there acquire some dignity under the guise of that affection, sent him these verses in letters close, indicating that he should not break the seal except in the presence of the Lord Pope, and this is how things turned out. Here are the verses:

Sole head of the world, O Rome,
you who've caused us to stray far from home
and plunged all your pastors
in stormy disasters,
greet Walter, who comes here on loan,
of women a wretched despiser.
Let the Curia now be the wiser:
to speak truth unriddled,
his fair lord he diddled
not once, as the young lad's adviser,
while still Homer's verses brought tears
to his eyes, but long since, in those years
when a beard full and rough
made him far tougher stuff,
and the long march of days stilled his fears.

When the archbishop learned of this, he cut off Master Walter from his company. Knowing that he had incurred the wrath of his lord, Walter took thought how he might regain his love. He began and composed this book to his honor and praise, comparing his virtues to those of Alexander, and so this is the reason why

6. On William, see J.R. Williams, "William of the White Hands and Men of Letters," in *Anniversary Essays in Medieval History by Students of C.H. Haskins* (Boston: Houghton Mifflin, 1929), 365–87.

he treated the narratives of Alexander rather than those of some other noble man. But some say that the reason for the work is that Master Matthew of Vendôme and Master Walter quarreled as to who wrote better poetry, and in contest with each other they composed the *Tobias* and the *Alexandreis*.[7]

William made Walter a canon, variously of Amiens, Beauvais, Reims, or Orléans, depending on the gloss one follows. Walter died of leprosy, or perhaps of self-flagellation;[8] if of leprosy, perhaps contracted from a prostitute.

In addition to the confusing and contradictory details drawn from the biographical notices, Walter is sometimes identified with a Walter of Lille who appears in the letters of John of Salisbury as a trusted emissary of King Henry II.[9] Colker, following Williams, denies this connection, while Pritchard is more equivocal on the matter.[10] Walter certainly wrote, in addition to his epic and his accentual poems, a long prose *Tractatus contra Judaeos*, a treatise of refutation against the Jews.[11] From Walter's own prose prologue to the *Alexandreis*, we know that he worked on the poem for five years. The biographical glosses assert that he began it in the year of Thomas Becket's death, 1170, but as William became Archibishop of Reims only in 1176, this is impossible. The exact dating of the poem is probably beyond definitive establishment, despite recent and sometimes contentious attempts to do so. The details of which we can be sure are as follows. (1) The poem cannot have been completed before 1176, when William was raised to the archbishopric of Reims. (2) The poem is referred to by Johannes de Hauvilla in the *Architrenius*, which is securely datable to 1184.[12] (3) It was well enough known by 1189 for lines 10.448–50 (10.537–39 of the translation) to have served as the model for the epitaph of Henry II.[13]

(4) A *prosimetrum* by Walter that was probably written between 1174 and 1176 refers to *opuscula* among which Alexander is a subject. Perhaps

7. Quoted by Colker, xv–xvi.

8. On the possible causes of Walter's death, see F. Châtillon, "Flagello sepe castigatus vitam terminavit: Contribution à l'étude des mauvais traitements infligés à Gautier de Châtillon," *Révue du Moyen Âge Latin* 7 (1951), 151–74.

9. *The Letters of John of Salisbury*, vol. 2, ed. W.J. Millor and C.N.L. Brooke (Oxford: Clarendon Press, 1979), Letters 161 (pp. 76 and 78), 168 (p. 114), 180 (pp. 192–96), and 189 (pp. 254–56).

10. Colker, *Alexandreis*, xvi–xvii; Williams, "William of the White Hands," 374–76; R. Telfryn Pritchard, trans., *The Alexandreis* (Toronto: Pontifical Institute of Mediaeval Studies, 1986), 2–3.

11. Patrologia Latina 209, cols. 459–574.

12. Johannes de Hauvilla, *Architrenius*, ed. and trans. Winthrop Wetherbee, Cambridge Medieval Classics 3 (Cambridge: Cambridge University Press, 1995), xxx.

13. Heinrich Christensen, *Das Alexanderlied Walters von Châtillon* (Halle: Waisenhaus, 1905), 10.

the *opuscula* on Alexander are in fact a draft of the *Alexandreis* still in progress. The *prosimetrum* contains twelve lines that recur virtually *verbatim* at 3.140–57 (3.169–89 of this translation), and there is reason, though not conclusive evidence, for believing that the epic's version of these lines is the earlier.[14] (5) Alan of Lille denigrates the *Alexandreis* in *Anticlaudianus* 1.166–70;[15] but the usual date of Alan's poem, 1182 or 1183, is in fact deduced from a presumed dating of the *Alexandreis* to 1181, so that it is of no use to us as evidence for the date of the latter. We can say nothing with certainty beyond the fact that the poem was probably begun no earlier than 1171 and was finished by about 1181, though most scholars until the last decade followed Christensen's suggestion of 1178–82.[16] Recently, Carlotta Dionisotti has argued for 1171–76, while Neil Adkin has insisted that the coronation of Alexander is intended to reflect the circumstances surrounding Philip Augustus' succession to the throne of France in late 1179.[17]

Receptions of the Text

Alan of Lille's criticism of the poem, the 1184 reference in the *Architrenius*, and the imitation of lines from the end of Book Ten in the epitaph of Henry II testify to the speed with which Walter's poem began to establish itself in the literary culture of its day. It created a vogue in the ensuing years for classicizing epics, notably the *Ylias* of Joseph of Exeter and the *Philippidos* of Guillaume le Breton (as distingushed from the more allegorical or satirical epics that abounded in twelfth-century Latin literature). The explosion of manuscripts in the thirteenth century assured the work's wide availability up to the date of the first printed edition. In the thirteenth century, Eberhard's *Laborintus* and Hugo of Trimberg's *Registrum multorum auctorum* listed the poem among standard school texts, while Henry of Ghent compained that it had displaced the reading of the classical poets in grammatical study.[18] The influential Latin verse anthology known as the

14. Carlotta Dionisotti, "Walter of Châtillon and the Greeks," in Peter Godman and Oswyn Murray, eds., *Latin Poetry and the Classical Tradition: Essays in Medieval and Renaissance Literature* (Oxford: Clarendon Press, 1990), 90–96.

15. Alan of Lille, *Anticlaudianus*, ed. R. Bossuat (Paris: J. Vrin, 1955).

16. Christensen, *Das Alexanderlied*, 4–13.

17. Dionisotti, "Walter of Châtillon"; Neil Adkin, "The Proem of Walter of Chatillon's *Alexandreis*: 'Si . . . nostros uixisset in annos,'" *Medium Aevum* 60 (1991), 207–21, and "The Date of Walter of Châtillon's *Alexandreis*," *Bolletino di Studi Latini* 22 (1992), 282–87.

18. "The *Alexandreis* is today held in such honor in the grammar schools that on its account the reading of the ancient poets is neglected" (my translation). Cited by Colker, *Alexandreis*, xx.

Florilegium Gallicum, a collection that began its life in northwestern France in the twelfth century, favors excerpts from the *Alexandreis* among its largely classical contents.[19] Henry of Avranches, arguably the most successful Latin poet of his generation, listed Walter alongside Homer and Lucan as one of the authors with whom he had to vie in order to give worthy honor to Oswald of Northumbria, the subject of a hexameter saint's life he wrote in the 1220s.[20] The prologue to Henry's life of Guthlac is closely modeled on the invocation of Walter's poem, while in Henry's *magnum opus*, a life of Francis, he uses the initials of his fourteen books to spell out the name of his patron, GREGORIUS NONUS, in imitation of Walter's practice, and he prefaces each book with four lines of summary, just as Walter had provided ten lines of *capitula* for each of his ten books.[21] The *Alexandreis* was translated into Old Norse, Czech, Dutch, and Spanish; Ulrich von Eschenbach and Rudolf von Ems drew on it substanitally for their Alexander romances.[22] It has been suggested that Petrarch composed his *Africa* as a kind of literary rebuttal of Walter's work.[23] If far less obvious among the Latin texts referred to by Chaucer than the *Consolation of Philosophy* or the *Dissuasio Valerii*, the *Alexandreis* was nevertheless among those works that Chaucer expected a sophisticated reader to recognize in passing allusions. In the Wife of Bath's prologue, for example, Alisoun refers (lines 503–5) to the tomb of Darius, "which that Appelles wroghte subtilly," an unmistakable reference to the ecphrasis, or formal description, of Darius' tomb in Book Seven.

Sources, Style, and Meaning

In his prose prologue, Walter points out that none of the classical poets had attempted a full epic treatment of the life and exploits of Alexander. What *had* come down to the twelfth century was a range of texts of vary-

19. Rosemary Burton, *Classical Poets in the Florilegium Gallicum* (Frankfurt am Main: Peter Lang, 1983); see p. 405 for an index entry to further references.

20. David Townsend, ed., "Henry of Avranches: *Vita Sancti Oswaldi*," *Mediaeval Studies* 56 (1994), 28–29 (lines 18–27).

21. For the prologue of Henry's life of Guthlac, see Neil Adkin, "The Proem of Henry of Avranches' *Vita S. Guthlaci*," *Analecta Bollandiana* 108 (1990), 349–55; Henry's life of Francis is edited in *Analecta Franciscana* 10 (1926–41), 405–521.

22. George Cary, *The Medieval Alexander*, ed. D.J.A. Ross (Cambridge: Cambridge University Press, 1956; repr. 1967), 64–67.

23. Thomas G. Bergin and Alice S. Wilson, trans., *Petrarch's Africa* (New Haven, Conn.: Yale University Press, 1977); see Bergin and Wilson's note on 8.186.

ing date and authorship.[24] Among these were several late imperial works: the narrative by Julius Valerius; a purported letter of Alexander to Aristotle on the marvels of India, much expanded in the early Middle Ages; a report of Alexander's contacts with the Indian Brahmins; and another text representing his correspondence with their king. Julius Valerius' text was epitomized in the ninth century. In the tenth, the vastly popular text most widely known as the *Historia de preliis*, the history of Alexander's battles, was first produced, but by the late twelfth century, in the course of its wide dissemination, it had undergone a series of subsequent recensions.[25] In the twelfth century there appeared a Latin version of an eighth-century Syriac work, the *Secreta secretorum*, which purports to be Aristotle's advice to Alexander on the practice of kingship.

In addition to these highly fictionalized narratives and ancillary texts, more properly historical accounts had come down to Walter's day, including the relevant sections of Orosius' universal history. But Walter drew principally on the Alexander biography of the early imperial author Quintus Curtius Rufus.[26] The work of Curtius was not as widely known as the *Historia de preliis*, and it survived in imperfect form, lacking the first two of its ten books. An interpolated version of the text survives, however, that fills in for the missing two books amidst other innovations, and it is in this supplemented form that Walter used the text.[27]

Walter's extensive debt to Curtius is obvious from a comparison of the poem with his principal source. Many details of the narrative can be easily traced to his model—the apparatus of sources at the bottom of the page in Colker's edition gives a quick index of the correspondences—and substantial portions of the poem turn Curtius' prose into verse with some relatively slight rearrangement and substitution of metrically apt vocabulary. The twentieth-century reader's instinct has been to see Walter's debts to Curtius and other sources as mitigating his artistry: modernist sensibility looks for creativity in an originality more absolute than twelfth-century literary culture expected or even esteemed. Medieval attitudes toward lit-

24. Cary, *The Medieval Alexander*, 24–70.

25. R. Telfryn Pritchard has translated one recension of the text: *The History of Alexander's Battles: Historia de preliis—The J1 Version* (Toronto: Pontifical Institute of Mediaeval Studies, 1992).

26. *Quintus Curtius*, trans. and ed. John C. Rolfe, Loeb Classical Library, 2 vols. (Cambridge, Mass.: Harvard University Press, 1962); *Quintus Curtius Rufus*, trans. John Yardley and Waldemar Heckel (Harmondsworth: Penguin, 1984).

27. Edme R. Smits, "A Medieval Supplement to the Beginning of Curtius Rufus's Historia Alexandri: An Edition with Introduction," *Viator* 18 (1987), 89–124.

erary craft were both more workmanly and more indebted to the classical rhetorical tradition, in which *inventio*, the discovery or appropriation of material, was only the first division of the poet's task: manuals of poetic practice that flourished in the generations just after the composition of the *Alexandreis* give invention very short treatment indeed, compared to their vast attentions to arrangement and style.[28]

Neither would medieval readers have been troubled—indeed, they would more likely have been gratified—by Walter's frequent and unacknowledged appropriations of phrases from the classical poets, most notably from Vergil, Ovid, and Lucan, but also from Horace, Juvenal, and the fifth-century Claudian, among others.[29] This splicing of voices from the long tradition of Latin verse was commonplace in medieval poetic practice. Walter's artistry is enabled, not compromised, by such interweavings of other texts into his own. For readers at the turn of the twenty-first century, this poetic practice, in which sampling and reappropriation play so large a part, is at once strange and strangely familiar. It challenges modernist notions of an unproblematic link between creativity and individual genius. For that very reason, though, it resonates with notions of intertextuality and postmodernism, notions that have percolated increasingly into our own sensibilities over the past twenty years. One might argue that Walter exploits the fertility of such recombinatory literary practice to the full. He produces his text as a tissue of other texts, in which his own voice emerges from the web of borrowed voices spun by his poem.[30]

The very fact that Walter has recast a prose biography as epic is the most fundamental level at which we can see this aesthetic of disjunction and juxtaposition operating. The poem abounds in incongruities between form and content produced by this amalgamation of genres. Such hybridizations are evident, for example, at points when characters speak in styles that have more in common with the extended, rhetorically balanced speeches of prose historiography than with the generally briefer and more focused dicta of epic characters. The speech of the doomed Darius to his

28. See for example the widely read *Poetria nova* of Geoffrey of Vinsauf, translated by Margaret F. Nims (Toronto: Pontifical Institute of Mediaeval Studies, 1967).

29. H. Christensen, *Das Alexanderlied*, 195–211; Otto Zwierlein, *Der Prägende Einfluss des antiken Epos auf die "Alexandreis" des Walter von Châtillon* (Mainz: Akademie der Wissenschaften und der Literatur, 1987).

30. For applications of postmodernist theory to the poem, see David Townsend, "*Mihi barbaries incognita linguae*: Other Voices and Other Visions in Walter of Châtillon's *Alexandreis*," *Allegorica* 12 (1992), 21–37, and "Sex and the Single Amazon in Twelfth-Century Latin Epic," *University of Toronto Quarterly* 64 (1995), 255–73. The observations in the following paragraphs reflect the arguments advanced in those essays.

men at 6.350–421 is an apogee of such ornate rhetoric. That the speech leaves his men cold is, to be sure, due principally to the fact that he has just invited them to participate in a suicide mission. Yet their reaction is also an index of how unsatisfactorily such a style incites men to arms upon the battlefield of epic. At other points, tactical deliberations of strategy admit of too much practical warcraft, and of too little individual heroism, to fit within an epic ethos of individual combat.

Other splicings suggest still further voices, and sensibilities more characteristic of still other genres. A description of the Greeks plundering the Persian camp in Book Three includes some lines (267–72) whose tone and diction vividly suggest the Roman satire tradition and its medieval continuations. The text passes thence to a description of Persian women raped by their Greek captors, and here the graphic sexuality shocks both for its brutality and for its transgression of epic norms. In Book Two, the description of the hill that Darius climbs for a view of his vast army (351–67) rather peculiarly imports the imagery of pastoral into the immediate martial context.

While a modernist reader might view such incongruities as compromising the poem's quality, the text actually goes out of its way to exploit them. The tomb ecphrasis of Book Four (222–342) powerfully flouts the norms of epic diction. Alexander has had the monument built for the body of Darius's wife, who has died in captivity. The sepulchre is decorated by a Hebrew sculptor named Apelles. At the beginning of the passage, we learn in passing that the names of Greek kings are set upon the tomb, but the next hundred lines are taken up by an unadorned list of scenes from the Hebrew Bible that occupy the monument's surface. The passage's bald, paratactic style, so starkly at odds with the norms of classical ecphrasis, has earned the censure of a number of twentieth-century critics.[31] But it is precisely this passage that garnered an inordinate degree of attention from many of the poem's medieval glossators; mnemonic verses were even composed in order to help students remember the arrangement of the representation. These lines held clear pride of place in medieval receptions of Walter's work.[32] Modern readers tend to get stuck on the passage's transgression of epic style and sensibility; but in the twelfth and thirteenth centuries, the ecphrasis may have evoked a very different use of language, namely the captions that often accompanied the pictorial cycles of murals, tapestries,

31. Townsend, "Other Voices," 21–22.
32. Ibid., 22–23. See the notes on 4.222–342 below.

and other media. Similarly, the ecphrasis of another tomb decorated by Apelles, that of Darius himself in Book Seven, evokes the legends on the great *mappae mundi* of the thirteenth and fourteenth centuries, such as the Hereford Map.[33] These ecphrases, and particularly that in Book Four, pass beyond the splicing of other acceptably literary genres into the epic. Here the text ceases to behave like high literature at all. Such passages have the potential to call into question the very boundaries by which we delineate "literature" from other uses of language that are culturally less prestigious.

Such effects are not merely a matter of style superficially conceived. "Style," as Jacques Lacan put it, "is the person to whom I am speaking";[34] it is also the means by which the text shapes us into the sorts of readers it requires, and so, through the medium of its discourse, affects our vision of the world. The *Alexandreis* demands readers who can negotiate the leaps between the disparate kinds of language it deploys, and who are wary of the discrepancies between those languages. At this level, the *Alexandreis* treats among its themes the very processes of reading and interpretation. Alexander himself interprets the world around him. In Book One, he reads flawlessly the crumbling traces of fallen Troy in the wastes of Asia Minor (530–70). But almost immediately thereafter, he betrays a very superficial and self-obsessed understanding indeed of a vision of the Hebrew High Priest, who appears to him in a dream as he prepares to march against the Persian Empire. In Book Two, when he attempts to undo the Gordian Knot (84–101), he shows more concern about how those around him will interpret his failure than about the action itself. In Book Ten, Satan commits the greatest interpretive gaffe of all, imagining that Alexander's threatened invasion of the Antipodes will be the fulfillment of the prophecy according to which some New Man will harrow Hell (154–59). In all these cases, interpreters of the Text that is the world around them fail to understand the signs confronting them because they insist on reading those signs according to inappropriate frames of reference.

But inadequate frames of reference are all we are given as readers. There is no Final Say in the *Alexandreis*. Each of its voices, each of the textual frames it evokes, is crossed by the others, to the point that even its most straightforwardly moralizing asides, which ought to resolve our doubts and to reestablish us in comfortable certitude, become suspect.

33. Christina Ratkowitsch, *Descriptio picturae: Die literarische Funktion der Beschreibung von Kunstwerken in der lateinischen Grossdichtung des 12. Jahrhunderts* (Vienna: Verlag der Österreichischen Academie der Wissenschaften, 1991), 164–73.

34. Jacques Lacan, *Écrits* (Paris: Éditions du Seuil, 1966), 9.

Ultimately, our attention wanders from the center of these utterances, toward the margins they form with respect to one another, and to the peripheries beyond them all. In Book Eight, toward the end of his wanderings, Alexander receives visits from the Queen of the Amazons and a messenger of the Scythians, whose societies clearly remain beyond his comprehension. Alexander's answer to the Scythian's indictment of his rapacity is to invade and subdue the speaker's land. But what the Scythian has prophesied about such a conquest, we can well imagine coming true: the displaced Scythians will attack from the margins of the Greeks' awareness, appearing where their incursions are least expected. And ultimately, as readers of a Text they understand very imperfectly indeed, the Greeks will lose what they have gained.

Walter clearly intended his epic as a poem for the ages, not merely for his own day. This is evident not only in the tenor of his prose prologue, but also in his decision to frame the text with ten lines of verse *capitula* at the head of each book. Such versified summaries were by Walter's day a fixture of manuscripts of the classical epics. By supplying them himself, Walter signals that this is a poem worthy of repeated reading and intense study. To limit the text's meaning to the concerns of its immediate historical milieu, however illuminating its original circumstances may be as a partial explication of the poem's significance, is thus finally an inadequate approach. But it is worth noting that Walter lived amidst his culture's sustained dreams of a New World Order, as contradictory as those dreams were, and as violent as were their conflicts with one another. The papacy was embarked upon a centuries-long campaign for sovereignty on earth as in heaven; the Holy Roman Emperor and the kings of France and England were just as determined to protect their own hegemony.[35] The text decries (7.360–63) the murder of Thomas Becket in 1170, one of the central symbols of that struggle between disparate dreams of mastery. The ideology of a Christendom united against an external enemy was shored up by the disastrous exploits of the Crusades, which had reached a lull when Walter wrote, but which would soon erupt again, as the earliest manuscripts were copied, in the Third and Fourth Crusades of 1189–92 and 1200–1204, respectively.[36]

35. For introductions to the struggle of church and secular authority in the High Middle Ages, see Geoffrey Barraclough, *The Medieval Papacy* (London: Thames and Hudson, 1968) and Brian Tierney, *The Crisis of Church and State, 1050–1350* (Englewood Cliffs, N.J.: Prentice-Hall, 1964).

36. For a general history of the Crusades, see Steven Runciman, *A History of the Crusades*, 3 vols. (Cambridge: Cambridge University Press, 1951–54, repr. 1987); on the Fourth

At the end of Book Five, Walter effuses that a king of the Franks as effective as the uncorrupted Alexander might well assure the defeat of Islam. But in a poem like the *Alexandreis*, Walter's panegyric only invites a further question. At what point can we say that Alexander is wholly uncorrupted? And why are we told that all the world *would* beg baptism at the hands of the Archbishop of Reims *if* the Franks had so worthy a king? Ultimately, Walter's text corrodes not only the hermeneutic certainty of our literary frames of reference, but also any illusions we might have about the unity of moral vision with which a great twelfth-century writer regarded the General Text in which he himself was embedded.

The Translation

I have consulted Gugger's seventeenth-century edition of the poem as reprinted in vol. 209 of the Patrologia Latina and Mueldener's 1863 edition, as well as Colker's currently standard text. My choice among variant readings sometimes diverges from Professor Colker's, and occasionally the translation reflects an understanding of the text different from that implied by Colker's punctuation. The translation is given its own lineation, but for easier reference to Colker's edition, I follow his paragraph divisions. Each paragraph begins with the corresponding line number of the Latin text in square brackets.

I hope that this version will convey something of the pleasure of reading the original text. I have aimed to afford the general anglophone reader a satisfying literary experience of the poem. At times, loyalty to spirit superseded loyalty to letter. I have not departed without hesitation from the syntax and vocabulary of the Latin, but in a number of ways, I tried to balance the claims of literal accuracy against those of the aesthetic effects, at least as I perceive them, of the original. As is the case with every translation, the one I offer here is already an interpretation. The student who wants to construct an argument around a close reading of Walter's text will have to check his or her claims against the original, or at least against R. Telfryn Pritchard's more literal prose version of 1986. One of my fond-

---

Crusade specifically, see John Godfrey, *1204, The Unholy Crusade* (Oxford: Oxford University Press, 1980).

est hopes is that this translation might persuade a few readers to acquire sufficient Latin of their own to get to Walter more directly.

Most notably, the reader may occasionally catch lines closely reminiscent of (if not directly lifted from) canonical English works. If Walter's verse is sometimes a tissue of allusions to the classical Latin poets, as a glance at Colker's *apparatus fontium* quickly reveals, I hope that my own occasional splicings into the English version will approximate the effect that Walter's uses of Vergil, Ovid, Lucan, Horace, and Claudian would have had on cultured twelfth-century readers. Such borrowed lines only loosely reflect the original; in some cases, their addition is gratuitous. I hope they hint at the anonymous fluidity of medieval Latin versification, a fluidity epitomized by Walter's own plethora of appropriated voices. And if this English version of Walter sounds occasionally like Shakespeare or Milton, perhaps it is in part because Shakespeare and Milton sound at points something like Walter.

Less radically, I freely recast the original syntax when a smooth English rendering demanded it. Sometimes I omitted modifiers or concurrent synonyms that struck me as pleonastic. In some passages, where Walter repeats the same word in close succession or rings inflectional changes on it, the repetition seemed monotonous rather than emphatic in the English, and I translated with synonyms instead.

I chose to translate the *Alexandreis* into blank verse because I wanted to render the poem in the meter that in English literature holds the same place as the dactylic hexameter holds in Latin. A few words on specific metrical practices are in order, beginning with the nature of the Latin verse form itself. The dactylic hexameter is the meter of the epics of Homer, Vergil, and the Silver Latin epic poets, as well as of Ovid's *Metamorphoses*. The bulk of medieval Latin verse is also composed in this meter, and not in the accentual forms Walter employed elsewhere (and that we associate with the secular and satirical verse best known today from the *Carmina Burana*, as set to music by Carl Orff). The hexameter is a flexible line, in which a foot of two long syllables, the spondee, can be substituted freely for the dactyl (a long and two shorts) in the first four feet, though the last two feet of the line are almost invariably a dactyl followed by a spondee. Since it is length of syllable, rather than stress, that determines the metrical pattern, the line allows considerable subtlety and variation in the ways these two effects clash or coincide. *Caesura*, the fall of word-ending in the midst of a foot, especially as a principal break in the second, third, or fourth foot of the line, constitutes one of the most carefully controlled aspects of the form. Medieval practice was looser than its Roman antecedents, but Walter adheres more closely to classical standards than do many of his contemporaries.[37]

The five-foot iambic line holds as central a place in the tradition of English verse as does the hexameter in Latin. But its practice varies as markedly across the centuries, from Chaucer's narrative poems, through Shakespeare, Milton, Pope, and the Romantics, to poets of our own century, as does Latin verse from Vergil to the humanist scholars of the sixteenth century and beyond. In the present translation, the reader will find a range of technical styles sometimes reminiscent of Renaissance or Baroque practice, sometimes more akin to second-string Victorians like Swinburne, sometimes bearing the conversational and rhythmically freer stamp of twentieth-century poetry. Occasional lines employ a trochaic rather than an iambic meter; feminine cadences often appear, with a final weak syllable after the last stress, or in some cases two weak syllables, so that the line approximates a six-foot Alexandrine. All these practices are amply attested in the English canon. They can also be seen as paralleling, in a general sense, the liberties and exceptions to strict practice that we find in medieval hexameters—and indeed sometimes in the classical poets themselves. In the translation, some words are scanned variously, depending on their position in the line, for example, "Darius," which needs sometimes to be read as two syllables, sometimes as three.

For the most part, I give proper names in their well-known English forms—"Aristotle" rather than "Aristoteles," for example, and "Ptolemy" rather than "Ptolomaeus" or "Tolomeus." I usually use the classical spelling of names that appear with a medievalized orthography in the Latin text, for example, "Euphrates" rather than "Eufrates." Biblical names appear in the forms of the Authorized Version, rather than in those of the Vulgate used by Walter. Now and then, a proper name in the original becomes a common noun in the translation, and vice versa. The index at the end of the volume is keyed to names as they appear in the translation, not in the original text.

I have kept explanatory notes to a minimum, trying to provide brief but serviceable elucidations of points the general reader might find confusing. A number of the notes are translated directly from medieval glosses extant in the manuscripts, so that the reader may develop some sense of

37. Paul Klopsch provides a thorough account of medieval metrical practice in *Einführung in die Mittellateinische Verslehre* (Darmstadt: Wissenschaftliche Buchgesellschaft, 1972).

how his or her own desires for clarification may parallel those of readers far closer in time to Walter's own day. When I opt for greater fullness in the notes, it is generally to include a medieval gloss that I consider especially interesting. Such glosses of course reflect medieval understandings rather than modern historicist scruples, and they should be taken as such: the note on 1.322, for example, records a thirteenth-century academic's fantasy, not the historical organization of Athens in the fourth century B.C.E.

Select Bibliography

Adkin, Neil. "The Date of Walter of Châtillon's *Alexandreis*." *Bolletino di Studi Latini* 22 (1992), 282–87.

———. "The Proem of Walter of Châtillon's *Alexandreis*: 'Si . . . nostros uixisset in annos.'" *Medium Aevum* 60 (1991), 207–21.

———. "The Proem of Henry of Avranches' *Vita S. Guthlaci*." *Analecta Bollandiana* 108 (1990), 349–55.

Cary, George. *The Medieval Alexander*. Ed. D.J.A. Ross. Cambridge: Cambridge University Press, 1956, repr. 1967.

Châtillon, F. "Flagello sepe castigatus vitam terminavit: Contribution à l'étude des mauvais traitements infligés à Gautier de Châtillon." *Révue du Moyen Âge Latin* 7 (1951), 151–74.

Christensen, Heinrich. *Das Alexanderlied Walters von Châtillon*. Halle: Waisenhaus, 1905. Repr. Hildesheim: Georg Olms, 1969.

Colker, Marvin. "Note on the History of the Commentary on the Alexandreis." *Medium Aevum* 28 (1959), 97–98.

DeCesare, R. *Glosse latine e antico-francese all' "Alexandreis" di Gautier de Châtillon*. Milan: Vita e Pensiero, 1951.

Curtius (Quintus Curtius Rufus). *Quintus Curtius*. Trans. and ed. John C. Rolfe. Loeb Classical Library. 2 vols. Cambridge, Mass.: Harvard University Press, 1962.

———. *Quintus Curtius Rufus*. Trans. John Yardley and Waldemar Heckel. Harmondsworth: Penguin, 1984.

Destombes, M. "The *mappaemundi* of the Poem *Alexandreidos* by Gautier de Châtillon." *Imago Mundi* 19 (1965), 10–12.

Dionisotti, Carlotta. "Walter of Châtillon and the Greeks." In *Latin Poetry and the Classical Tradition: Essays in Medieval and Renaissance Literature*, 73–96. Ed. Peter Godman and Oswyn Murray. Oxford: Clarendon Press, 1990.

Giordano, Carlo. *Alexandreis: Poema di Gautier da Châtillon*. Naples: P. Federico & G. Ardia, 1917.

Greenia, George. "The *Alexandreis* and the *Libro de Alixandre*: Latin versus Vernacular Direct Discourse." Dissertation, University of Michigan, 1984.

Harich, Henriette. *Alexander Epicus: Studien zur Alexandreis Walters von Châtillon*. Graz: Verlag für die Technische Universität Graz, 1987.

Harvey, P.D.A. *Medieval Maps*. Toronto: University of Toronto Press, 1991.

Hellegouarc'h, J. "Un poète latin du xiie siècle: Gautier de Lille, dit Gautier de Châtillon." *Bulletin de l'Association Guillaume Bude* 4th ser. (1967), 95–115.

Jolly, W.T. "The Alexandreid of Walter of Châtillon. A Translation and Commentary." Dissertation Tulane University, 1968.

Knapp, Fritz Peter. *Similitudo: Stil- und Erzählfunktion von Vergleich und Exempel in der lateinischen, französischen und deutschen Grossepik des Hochmittelalters*, 222–67. Vienna and Stuttgart: W. Braumüller, 1975.

Kratz, Dennis. *Mocking Epic: Waltharius, Alexandreis, and the Problem of Christian Heroism*. Madrid: J.P. Turanzas, 1980.

———, trans. *The Romances of Alexander*. New York: Garland, 1991.

Lafferty, Maura Keyne. "Reading Latin Epic: Walter of Châtillon's *Alexandreis*." Dissertation, University of Toronto, 1992.

———. "Mapping Human Limitations: The Tomb Ecphrases in Walter of Châtillon's *Alexandreis*." *Journal of Medieval Latin* 4 (1994), 64–81.

———. *Epic and the Problem of Historical Understanding in Walter of Châtillon's Alexandreis*. Forthcoming.

Lefèvre, Yves. "Gautier de Châtillon, poète complet." In *Alain de Lille, Gautier de Châtillon, Jakmart Giélée, et leur temps*, 229–48. Ed. H. Roussel and F. Suard (Lille: Presses Universitaires de Lille, 1980).

Meter, Glynn. *Walter of Châtillon's Alexandreis Book 10—A Commentary*. Frankfurt am Main: Peter Lang, 1991.

Pritchard, R. Telfryn, trans. *The History of Alexander's Battles: Historia de preliis—The J1 Version*. Toronto: Pontifical Institute of Mediaeval Studies, 1992.

Raby, F.J.E. *A History of Secular Latin Poetry in the Middle Ages*. 2nd ed. Vol. 2. Oxford: Clarendon Press, 1957.

Ratkowitsch, Christine. *Descriptio picturae: Die literarische Funktion der Beschreibung von Kunstwerken in der lateinischen Grossdichtung des 12. Jahrhunderts*. Vienna: Verlag der Österreichischen Academie der Wissenschaften, 1991.

Smits, Edme R. "A Medieval Supplement to the Beginning of Curtius Rufus's Historia Alexandri: An Edition with Introduction." *Viator* 18 (1987), 89–124.

Townsend, David. "*Mihi barbaries incognita linguae*: Other Voices and Other Visions in Walter of Châtillon's *Alexandreis*." *Allegorica* 12 (1992), 21–37.

———. "Sex and the Single Amazon in Twelfth-Century Latin Epic." *University of Toronto Quarterly* 64 (1995), 255–73.

Walter of Châtillon. *Galteri de Castellione Alexandreis*. Ed. Marvin Colker. Padua: Antenore, 1978.

———. *The Alexandreis*. Trans. R. Telfryn Pritchard. Toronto: Pontifical Institute of Mediaeval Studies, 1986.

———. *Alexandreis. Das Lied von Alexander dem Grossen*. Trans. Gerhard Streckenbach. Heidelberg: Lambert Schneider, 1990.

———.*Tractatus contra Judaeos*. Patrologia Latina 209, cols. 459–574.

———. *Die Lieder Walters von Châtillon in der Handschrift 351 von St. Omer*. Ed. Karl Strecker. Berlin: Weidmann, 1925.

———. *Moralisch-satirische Gedichte Walters von Châtillon*. Ed. Karl Strecker. Heidelberg: Carl Winter, 1929.

Wetherbee, Winthrop. *Platonism and Poetry in the Twelfth Century: The Literary Influence of the School of Chartres*. Princeton, N.J.: Princeton University Press, 1972.

Williams, J.R. "William of the White Hands and Men of Letters." In *Anniversary Essays in Medieval History by Students of Charles Homer Haskins*, 365–87. Ed. Charles Holt Taylor. Boston: Houghton Mifflin, 1929.

Zwierlein, Otto. *Der prägende Einfluss des antiken Epos auf die "Alexandreis" des Walter von Châtillon*. Mainz: Akademie der Wissenschaften und der Literatur, 1987.

THE
ALEXANDREIS

Prologue

It is a matter of time-honored custom, when anything new is recited in the ears of the multitude, that the mob habitually breaks up into various passions. One applauds and proclaims that what he's heard is praiseworthy. Another is led on by his ignorance, or else he is perverted by the prick of malice or hatred's tinder, to judge harshly even what is well spoken: he deems that well-turned verses must be returned to the anvil. It is amazing that the human race has been so distorted from its original nature—that nature by which all the things that God had created were very good—that it is more inclined to damn than to forgive, and finds it easier to distort what seems dubious than to put the better construction on such things. Long fearing this, I intended to suppress you forever, O my *Alexandreis*, and either to destroy outright a work of five years' labor, or at least to bury it in obscurity as long as I lived. At last I decided that I must bring you out into the light: thus at length you might dare come to public notice. Indeed, I hardly think myself superior to the bard of Mantua: though his works exceeded mortal capability, they were denigrated by the tongues of carping poets, who presumed to slander when he was dead one whom none among mortals equaled while he lived. But our Jerome, a man as distinguished for his eloquence as for his Christian piety, who was accustomed to answer his rivals in his various prefaces, makes it clear that among authors there remains no place of safety, since the goad of his competitors stung even a man of such acknowledged authority. But if, despite all this, some attraction will perhaps still entice readers to this little work, I wish to implore them, should they find anything flawed or worthy of ridicule in the volume, to consider the restricted brevity of the time in which we wrote it, and the loftiness of the material, which, as Servius attests, none of the ancient poets dared undertake for a thorough treatment. Let them keep this in mind, and so learn that things ought at least to be tolerated by indulgence that could be more strictly condemned, were one to judge according to the letter of the law. But enough of this. Now let us undertake what is at hand and mark out the whole work with chapter headings, so that the reader can more easily find what he is seeking.

Book One

The Headings of the First Book

Book One invests the king with arms and sceptre
when Aristotle's holy draught has filled him.
The line of Cecrops joins him once again.
Thebes' citadel he topples, with his fleet
crosses the deep, and from his ship claims Asia
by arrowshot. In bloodless victory
he spares the foe. Soul-proud, he thinks the realms
of all the world are his. From mountain peak
he views Asia, shares out his birthright cities.
Marveling at Troy, he tells the dreams he's seen.

Book One

How generously the Duke of Macedon
dispensed his wealth, with what a splendid host
he conquered Darius' and Porus' lands,
tell us, Muse; how Greece laughed in her triumph,
and once again to Corinth tribute came
home from the Persians—these are deeds well known
through all the earth. Had sufferance of the Fates
allowed this man to live till our own day,
unbroken by the ravages of age,
Fame never would have sung the victory-song
for Caesar, and all glory of Rome's race
would lie abject, the great blaze of his worth

engulfing that pale flame. The Wain's slow stars
would grow more languid still, and Lucifer
would turn pale at the rising of his sun.
[12] But you, whose royal forebears Britain vaunts,
be with me now, you who as bishop brought
to Sens no less praise than when Brennius
broke Rome with arms of Sens, and would have made
Tarpeius' citadel his own, had not
the silver goose roused those who should have watched.
When you at last had gained the see of Reims,
the warlike land lost any earlier name
for harshness. From the moment of your birth,
Philosophy took you as foster child:
she gave you milk of Helicon to drink,
laid bare the holy teaching of her heart,
and granted, scattering the veiling clouds,
that you who were long purged by study's fire
should penetrate the hidden cause of things.
Stay with me as I steer for open sea;
pour out the holy waters, and upon
your head set laurel—grant I may ascribe
to you the inspiration of my song.
[27] On that tender face down had not yet
sprouted, nor his mother's embrace been met
by a rough cheek unlike her own, before
the boy sought arms with undivided heart.
He heard that Darius with empire's yoke
burdened his father's lands, set laws for Greeks;
outraged, he couched his anger in these words:
"So overlong this childish holiday!
With flashing swordpoint shall I never be
allowed to strike the Persian yoke, head off
the fleeing tyrant's sluggish mount in swift
pursuit, and rout the dukes—though still a boy,
perhaps, at least in war to seem a man,
a helmet on my head, and on my banner
a lion fluttering? Did Hercules
not as a boy—no, in his very cradle!—
once overcome two monstrous serpents' force,

their jaws crushed shut? Great Aristotle's name
strikes fear in boyhood's years; for otherwise,
I'd scarcely hesitate to undertake
acts of like bravery. And besides, courage
is usually greater at the age of twelve,
though still the body's small, when green youth's force
grows ripe through such delay. But shall I always
be thought the offspring of Nectanabus?
Let no man call me bastard to my face!"

[48] And so he spoke, declaiming to his heart.
Just as a lion cub perhaps may see
deer in Hyrcanian fields, their antlers raised,
going to pasture, but as yet his strength
has not filled out his limbs—though neither are
teeth set, nor claws sharpened, he trembles, and
his untried tongue strikes at his teething palate;
more quickly with his courage he sheds blood
than with his fangs, but adult will atones
for small, slow feet—so also did the boy
cavort, all up in arms, though weak of hand
bearing the lion in his inmost heart,
and headlong daring outstripped his tender years.

[59] The master, pale and wan, his hair unkempt—
nor did his face poorly reflect his zeal—
had chanced to come forth from the chamber where
he'd armed his disputatious propositions,
and finished all the corpus of his Logic.
How difficult not to betray that zeal
in countenance! His darkened brow evinced
the midnight lamp; his skin clung to the bones
as thin as parchment; in his hands, starved wanness
impressed the joints. Truly the work of study
afflicts the limbs and outer flesh with hunger:
the inner man receives the nourishment.

[72] He saw the burning face of Philip's son—
its fiery redness betrayed his hidden ire—
and asked why his soul blazed, from whence had come
his grief, why such an angry fever raged.
The boy, in reverence for his mentor's face

cast down his gaze; fallen before his knees,
he poured the tale: his father's sad old age,
his native land oppressed by Darius' empire.
His anger mounted with his tears, until
he drank in eagerly his master's words:
"Put on a grown man's mind, boy, take up arms.
You have the stuff of virtue; bring its matter
to actuality. Lend me your ear—
I'll teach you how you may accomplish it.

[85] "Press these few precepts on your memory,
I charge you. Shun the wicked, double tongues
of princes' slaves; exalt none whom their nature
dictates should, rather, lie abject—the flood
torrential rains have swelled flows fiercer than
a steady river. So a slave who rises
to honor's peak and mastery's rank, when wealth
has been shared out, is deaf to all entreaty,
more vicious than a snake caught unawares.
Yet reason does not bar the will to raise
up those whom honesty marks out for praise,
whom high morals exalt, though they lack wealth
and land and lineage; for, to speak the truth,
gold robs from virtue more than it has added,
and nothing more corrupt exists among
the monstrous creatures of prodigious night.
He whom abundance of virtue marks out,
whom character extols, though poor, has that
which, preferable to gold, confers on him
high birth and beauty, and redeems the vice
which stains his land. True virtue's sought within:
he who abounds in inner moral strength
adorns his soul with true nobility.

[105] "If you should judge a suit, balance the scales
of Justice evenly. Let love not turn
your mind; beware lest your resolve be bent
by awe of persons or by flatterers' bribes.
A bribe received besmears the unjust judge;
a bribe indeed will cast aside his wit,
and plunge his mind into oblivion.

But once the raging pestilence of greed,
that mother of all vices, gains a hold
before the court, all semblance of virtue
is thrown in chains; the course of justice spurned
breeds crime, when courts care nothing for the laws.
Before a humble plea spare haughtiness.
[116] "Strike camp, draw up your troops, attack the foe.
Resolve and capability are one.
If unripe years cannot sustain the burden
that needs strong hands, when Mars plays out his game,
the troops at least should see you armed, and fighting
with good cheer, thundering with threats and prayers.
Sometimes a lord fights best through his commands.
For when fear strikes the tents, and when limp terror
lays low the ranks, when heart and hand are wavering,
if by his urging the commander slakes
his soldiers' ears, fear vanishes, and so
unchecked youth runs to arms, drowning its qualms.
Before all others press the retreating foe.
But if perhaps your soldiers run for camp,
fleeing the hostile ranks with backward step,
stand fast, the last to flee, and let them see
your delay; let it shame them to return
without their king. Meanwhile your eye shall scan
how many soldiers stand, how many ranks
of infantry are poured between the hills,
how many knights reflect the sun from shields
and helmets—let their numbers bring no fear!
Fall first to arms, mount first your charger, if
your followers advance half-heartedly.
Your energy and spirit should stand forth
preeminent, your burning soul, your skill
in Mars' fierce duel. To steed oppose your steed,
to sword your sword, to helmet and to shield
your own arms of like sort. And let the vanquished
scarce be permitted to accept defeat.
[144] "But entering a city, when the conquered
have made it over to you—or, should they
resist, when you have broken down its gates—

lay out its treasures, rain gifts on the troops,
pour generosity's oil upon the wounds
nursed, raw and swollen, by the sad of heart.
Anoint their flagging souls with proffered riches,
applying gold's elixir—such a balm
can cure the sad mind: thus wealth heals the poor,
and generosity the greedy man.
But if perhaps the means lie not at hand,
if wealth is lacking, or the treasure fails,
let love not be diminished, nor the wealth
of soul run short. Entice with promises,
and pay in season what you've earlier pledged.
Fear not to dull your palm with entertainment:
a gift may strengthen character, ensnare
the greedy, cover vice, raise up one's birth,
subdue the foe. They have no need of walls
whom generous hands protect; for whether peace
flourish, or discord rage throughout the world,
reigning upon the ruins of that peace,
their gifts stand as a fortress and a shield
for hesitant princes who fear some foe.
No arms nor walls protect a greedy duke.

[164] "What else should I advise? Do not grow soft
with wanton luxury; and let not love,
that sickness of the mind, which takes its joy
in murmured assignations, break your breast.
Though you have conquered others, you yourself
have passed beneath the victor's yoke, if Bacchus
and Venus find you ready to receive them.
The freedom of an idle soul dies mad;
the mind grows dull inside the forge of Venus.
Dire wars and quarrels rise from drunkenness,
which heaps a wretched tomb for failing Reason.
Thus love and wine sap upright character.
Scant will for pleasure ought to touch their minds
who set the laws of men and rule the world.
Let Justice, which your fathers' zeal extolled,
direct your actions too, and let Astraea,
the last among the gods to leave the earth,

be called back from the heavens. Brook no lack
of modesty, devotion, or respect
for the right path. Consult the gods' high will,
remain mild when petitioned, set your strength
upon the laws. According to the statutes
accuse the guilty. Until anger wanes
postpone vengeance, and do not nurse your hatred
after its blows. If thus you live, your name
shall stretch forever through eternity."

[184] His guardian thus instructed virtue's ward,
filling his open ear with fecund showers,
and pressing upright ways upon his heart.
His thirsty ears drank in the holy lore,
and willingly committed all he'd heard
to memory's inmost chamber: so his mind
burned feverishly, goaded on by praise;
the love of war and pomp took root within.
All fear departs now; now hope overcomes
his youth, his vow is made; now in his mind
against the enemy he rages; now
he reigns; now all the foursquare world serves him.
And so when that age came that frees the young
from the rod's strokes, the Macedonian took
up arms, not for himself, but for his land,
although a novice yet a giant in heart,
although a prince a citizen, and in
his breast a seasoned fighter. One might then
have seen Neoptolemus unsubdued,
desiring things even his sire Achilles
might scarce accomplish. And his frenzied rage
was ready now not only for the Persians,
against whom he directed a just quarrel;
he swore to take the whole world, should Fate grant it.

[203] There was a city, from its founder named
Corinth. Its very site, its greater wealth
of people and of stores, its kings' firm will,
decreed that it should stand as capital
and mother-city of the realm. This town,
its idols cast out by the Gospel's word,

Paul shepherded to fields of endless spring.
Here, then, the Macedonian took up
the sacred crown with reverence, lest after
his father's death he blunt the civic laws.
His ivory sceptre shone where princes flanked him;
on either side stood reverend white-haired fathers,
whose mild old age disposed the entire realm.
The bulwark of their counsel blocked sedition,
and in their tongues lay all their skill in war;
they had their care in arms they did not bear.
Some space apart from Alexander stood
those men of unchecked spirit, in whose breast
strength took command of skill, and to Achilles
Nestor conceded. Opposite the prince,
surrounded by the poets' unarmed flock,
sat Aristotle clad in flowing raiment,
endowed now with a staff, and bent by Fate,
which pressed his years; a wreath of plaited laurel
covered his unkempt locks. Such sights, the gaze
of princes, fed the Macedonian's strength;
his bold ferocity, though long since ripened,
now grew into the aspect of a king.
His ears and heart echoed the crowd's acclaim,
and everything he'd earlier conceived
his strength made wider, daring greater feats.
His countenance accorded with his soul;
his eyes showed forth his deep resolve, his face
was kindled. Thus one easily perceived
his rank, though royal finery he lacked—
the bright circlet of purest gold, the cloak
whose purple blazed with fire-bearing gems;
his reverend face alone bespoke a king.

[239] It was the month whose name's derived from youth,
when vines flower, which later will hang dense
with clustering grapes (so may the autumn drink,
and winter store its vintage). With its seed
the tall crop swelled, and Phoebus was preparing
to sear the scuttling Crab with lengthened rays,
when common acclamation of the dukes

and people raised the Macedonian
up to the throne, who to his countrymen
assigned their ranks in war. Of these, the knights
in number were four thousand and five hundred,
of varied age, though of one zeal in arms.
Not only youths did Alexander choose,
but those whose age stood witness to their prowess
under his father. Not one captain's years
were less than sixty: well might one have thought,
seeing them out of armor, that they formed
a peacetime senate, rather than the troop
of royal generals around their prince.
Besides these, he equipped as infantry
another thirty-two thousand, whose arms
included javelins and two-edged pikes,
and slings that cast forth stones with lethal torque,
swords, the bow that squanders life, and blades
of crescent shape, arrows that carry death.
They brandish spears and threatening, sharp stakes;
their helms and breastplates shield their necks and chests.
And virtue armed them all, virtue which stands
preeminent above all weapons; yet
I marvel that with men in such few numbers
the hero would desire the world's submission,
still more that he obtained it. Like some prodigy
of Fate stand these events, so many realms
submitting to the rule of this one man.

[268] Amidst the universal clash and din,
while all the world shook with so many rumors,
the town of Athens first withdrew support,
provoking war of doubtful outcome, and
opposing force with force. Demosthenes
had prompted this. The Macedonian
heard it and raged; he swiftly bade the Greeks
move camp. Thus unexpected, he approached
the foe, and laid siege to the city walls.
The senate, safe in Pallas' citadel,
meanwhile heard Aeschines accuse the strife
Demosthenes began: he argued that

no other rescue could be found than truce.
While both sides' embassies pursued the task
they'd taken up, the king was touched by love
to grant to his own land, now suppliant,
the rights of peace, and with mild countenance
to free that city for her native arts:
War's obligations troubled her no more.
[284] To ancient Thebes he sped thence, when he'd joined
unruly Athens to himself again.
The armed Boeotians manned the walls, crowned now
by lines of youths. They closed the gates to him
who wished to enter—had they shown a will
to take him as their lord, to meet him not
with arms but prayers, or had their fraud and crime
brought them more fitting shame, perhaps they could
have checked the torrent of his rage, gained grace,
and kept their former life; but since they dared
despise him as a king for his brief years,
they rightfully received the tyrant's strokes.
[295] Now, while the city's ruin held his mind,
the chieftains of the neighboring towns approached
that people stricken by such divers blows.
The whole race stood accused, as they recalled
a tribe intent from birth upon dire outrage,
and sodden with Greek blood: its ancestors
engendered by the serpent, venom poured
into descending generations' hearts.
"Who has heard nothing of Niobe's pride,
or of Agave, spattered with the blood
of her own son among the wailing women?
Who knows not of the fire that punished Semele,
or of that blinded king who shamefully
returned to his own source, of the twin sons
brought forth from that cursed union, whose strife
one with the other was all Europe's fall?"
[308] The prince's anger blazed to hear their words,
and straightaway he ordered an attack
to be prepared; then with a thousand knights
around the haughty town he thundered, while

atop the walls the citizens repelled them,
and from close quarters showered down their weapons.
The infantry, meanwhile, strove eagerly
to undermine the walls with sturdy mattocks
and levers jammed beneath; lest from above
their foes should drive them off, their comrades stood
to hand, joining their shields to ward the blows
like some great tortoise shell which kept them safe.
Already the foundations totter; now
the whole heap nears collapse; those who remain
among the living flee with a great leap,
and hide themselves in secret refuges.
But as the stones fell and their foes dropped back,
the Greeks made inroads through the wall. The whole
crowd surged into the city. None was spared
for tender age or sex, while Alexander
himself now stood at hand, girt with his arms,
and made attack upon the Theban town.
But trusty Cleades was there, to sing
the king a sweet song in these lyric strains:
"Bright Macedonian offspring of the gods,
bravest of kings, upon whom smile the stars,
to you the fateful sisters' hastening thread
grants all the climes of earth. Your eager breast
is armed with Aristotle's holy words
of caution, that, unconquered, you should spare
the humble vanquished, warring down the proud,
and them alone. O king, do you prepare
to raze this city wholly? From her sprang
that Bacchus whom all India extols
in shrines that smoke with redolent incense.
Did not this land rear gods, and also nurture
the sire of your ancestors, Hercules,
whose praise surpasses all throughout the world
your fathers often vanquished? See these walls
and turrets built by Amphion's sweet strains!
Learn pity toward the conquered, savagery
toward those alone who yet must be subdued.
The kingdom totters if no mercy shores it.

Yet if you will destroy the citizens,
then spare at least the soil; revere its gods."
[345] So Cleades fell silent; but the judgment
of Alexander held unwavering.
He loosened anger's reins, and ordered first
the walls and towers be leveled to the ground;
he smote what then remained with Vulcan's stroke.
[349] So Dirce's fields lay pressed by worthy vengeance;
Boeotia learned to serve its new-made king.
With home and native land thus well disposed,
the Macedonian prepared to thunder
against Darius. Those less skilled in arms,
less famous and less bold, he set aside,
and to these gave the Argive lands to guard.
Straightway he loaded ships with varied stores,
nor did he choose to employ in such a task
a few small skiffs, but in the swelling fleet
two hundred ships less eighteen made the count;
set loose, they strained towards the sea in flight.
Wings on their sails, no anchor gripped the sand,
and all departed from their homeland's port.
The strident voice of men foreboding ill
rose up to strike the heavens with wondrous cry,
the trumpets blared out with a mingled din,
and all the sea resounded. Inborn love
of native country, thus you draw us all!
What sweetness you contain! The speeding ships
bear off the nation's sons across the deep;
they hasten willingly to Persia's land.
Yet though their lord entices none to plundered
wealth against his will, sweet love of home
calls back the willing mind, and turns their eyes
and souls again to Argos' dwindling coast,
until the ridge of Europe and the port
from which they've come shrink from their longing gaze.
Such was the unchecked Macedonian's will
for warfare: he alone, forgetting both
mother and sisters, turned away his eyes
from Grecian soil, and rejoiced to see

the green Cilician fields and Asia's hills
rise up out of the deep, his narrow heart
scarcely containing happiness so great.
His joy contemned delay; he bade the oarsmen
lean to their task, nor trust the billowing sails.
No sluggards on the benches there—compliant,
they rose to lash the sea with many a blow.
[386] A sling might hurl its rapid-flying stones
just so far as the fleet stood out of port.
From there Pellaeus shot an arrow shaft
that struck the hostile land, while all the host
pronounced that wound a happy omen, and
bore to the stars their joyous shouts. Straightway
the anchor bit the sandy shore, and swiftly
they leapt to pitch a camp on the green strand.
They made a banquet there, and in their mirth
continued their libations through the night.
[396] The third part of the world now takes its name
from her to whom it paid obedience
in former times—men call it Asia. Near
the rising of the sun, it's bounded by
the whirl of Ocean; from the south, it stretches
northward to Lake Maeotis and the Tanais,
which close it off from Boreas' chill winds,
while our own sea divides its lands from Europe.
A fair division of the world would grant
to this region alone a full half-share:
though it be one of three, geographers
claim it divides the world in twain; and so
it does not envy the more central place
of the two continents of lesser breadth.
Such is the site of Asia: gentle growth
of forest shadows it, where rivers flow.
It glories in its various regions' praise.
The elephants of jeweled India shriek,
that country which sows twice and reaps as often.
The Caucasus arises to the north;
the scent of Paradise blows from the East.
Assyrians, Medes, and Persians hold the land

whose name is Parthia, now, and next to this
Mesopotamia stands, receiver of
the wealth of Babylon and the Chaldean realms.
Then come Arabian lands, made redolent
with incense of Sabaea: there that bird
is born, alone forevermore, the Phoenix,
despair of all logicians, while nearby,
the cinnamon and neighboring myrrh tree grow.
Euphrates on this side laps Syria's shores;
on that, Armenia, mindful of the Flood,
assails the heavenly realms above with threats.
Then over all the fields of Palestine
towers the one Judaea of one God,
and at the center of the earth, Jerusalem
is set, where, sprung from virgin womb, Life died,
nor was a reborn world content to stand,
but shuddered, stricken, at the death of God.
So many are the realms of Asia, that
my pen, recording all, must curb the list
or bring some tedium to readers' eyes.

[427] The birds made ready now to sing the dawn
and greet its growing light with gentle melody.
The day-star crossed the bounds of aged night,
hastening the stars' flight before the sun
on breathless steed, when Alexander raised
his limbs from easy sleep. And when he glimpsed
the dawning light reflected from the sea
in glimmering rays, he came out from the camp
at once, rushing to measure with his eyes
the lands of Asia from the mountain top.
From there he saw the waving fields of grain,
the woodland groves, the meadows of green grass,
illustrious cities fortified by walls,
the stalks of Bacchus, elm trees wed to vines,
and said, "Comrades, it is sufficient, now.
This one land is enough. To you I leave
our own country and Europe's narrow realm."
Thus he spoke, and to his generals
doled out his fathers' world. His confidence
in Fate was such, that now that scourge of princes

believed the earth's four quarters were his portion.
He cleared the fields of those who'd plunder them,
and turned aside the enemy's cattle raids.
He laid his course thence, claiming for himself
Cilicia's towns, and with the clemency
of a mild prince made peace with all those cities.
Such skill pleased Alexander more than debts
of blood paid out to Mars; and so he conquered,
yet spared his foes, as skilled in peace as war.
[452] His course flew thence through Phrygia's citadels,
toward Ilion—walls built on broken faith!—
and there he wandered the Idalian groves,
where wingèd Jove seized with betaloned feet
the comely boy of lovely mouth, bearing
his pleasing prize above the heaven's bounds.
While zealously he sought at least the trace
of ancient glory, there he came upon
Oenone's poplar, rooted by a stream
where the adulterer's blade had carved in stealth
his record: there one read of Paris' loves.
A thick-grown vale lies there, where as a jest
the case was tried in which the profligate
profaned the judgment. Thence flowed the first source
of Ilion's fall, the evil stain, and fire
upon Pergamum—now a meagre place.
And yet one may consider its past greatness
from present traces: ancient ruins witness
how vast the measure was of crumbling Troy.
[468] As thus the Macedonian slowly wandered
among so many tombs of Argive warriors,
their buried shades and ashes, whom inscriptions
still gave their titles clearly carved, behold!
He saw Achilles' tomb, of lesser breadth
than fame, adorned with verses such as these:
AEACUS SON HECTORS SLAYER I FELL
UNARMED UNWARY IN A HIDDEN SPOT
PIERCED THROUGH THE HEEL BY PARIS STEALTHY DART
The brevity of these words led the king
to vivid recollection of that prince,
and on the barren sands he poured pure wine.

He hastened to perfume the place with incense.
"O splendid fortune of this man," he cried,
"whose praises call to mind Maeonia's bard!
He dragged Hector, the land's chief strength and sire,
lifeless around the city's walls; and yet
this is the highest increase to his honor—
or so I judge—that such a man in death
should merit such a herald of his praise
as Homer. Would that Fame, unenvious,
should sing, when we are dead, such songs of praise!
Indeed, when all the world receives my laws—
when Atlas and the Ganges are subdued,
and Boreas and Ammon feel the strength
of Macedonia—when the broad earth
contents itself with but a single prince,
as with a single sun, one thing alone
I dread will fail my buried dust—lapsed fame,
which I would set before Elysian bliss.
[493] "Let Fortune not deter you from your course,
foresighted Greeks, though often she may proffer
a bitter lot—she who will not maintain
the same face very long. Unworthy, he
who shuns the harsh and bitter, to receive
the blandishments of gentle Fortune's smile.
I've seen what had been harsh, before, grow mild.
A hidden truth I set before you here,
so that you will not doubt through ignorance
where I've derived such store of confidence.
While mourning Greece bewept my father's death,
and when Pausanias had paid his debt,
slaughter for slaughter, one deep midnight, while
the stars urged sleep, I lay alone within
a privy chamber. Dream-filled torpor pressed
upon my fellows, but my breast was burned
by watchful care for whether I should guard
our native land, or rout its enemies.
In neither purpose resolute, inclined
toward both, I wavered in my new realm's course.
Lo, suddenly I saw the room grow bright,

saw heavenly radiance burst the doors, saw night's
darkness pressed back, and shadows turned to day.
While fear assailed by mind, and through my limbs
I felt the creeping witness of my dread,
there stood at hand (dare I to call him man?)
one from celestial regions, grave of mien,
whom barbarous garments clothed in varied hue.
A jeweled fringe grazed his flaming steps, and fillets
gleamed 'round his head, as on his course he passed.
A gold plate pressed upon his dewy locks.
Twelve gemstones burned with haughty light upon
his breast in pattern wondrous. On his brow,
four characters marked out, it seemed, some name;
but since his strange tongue was unknown to me,
I could not read it. A priest's diadem
sat on his head; his reverend foot lay hidden
beneath his pontiff's robes. I might have asked
what man he was, or why and whence he'd come,
had he not spoken first:
" 'Set out, most valiant Macedonian,
from your own land,' he said. 'To you I grant
dominion of each race; but if perchance
you see one like me come to meet you, spare
my people.' Thus he spoke, and, vanishing,
suffused the house with preternatural fragrance.
Proud band, you fight beneath such a commander."
With this he turned his steps back to the camp.

[539] Indeed he spoke the truth: for after Tyre
was overthrown, he neared Jerusalem
in victory amidst his many legions.
Great fear arose that he would desecrate
the Temple of the Lord; but then came forth,
in such robes as the king before had seen
upon that starry prelate, the High Priest,
flanked by the holy elders of the town,
to check the ire of the unvanquished prince.
As though in recognition, he leapt down
to venerate the priest, and bowed to earth.
All marveled that he paid the man such honor,

which always had been paid, rather, to him.
The king now passed within the city's walls
with only a few men, his legions stationed
beyond the gates. Then, as the Hebrews bade him,
he offered gifts of peace, and with great wealth
enriched the Temple. Thus he bade farewell;
Mars' strife was spared that holy city's folk,
whom he endowed with his continuing boon.

Book Two

The Headings of the Second Book

The second book leads Darius into battle.
He writes to Alexander, counts his troops.
The hero's sword cuts loose the fatal yoke.
Through Philip's care he rallies from disease.
Cilicia's narrow passes hem the battle lines.
The die of unjust Fate claims Sisenes.
The Persian dukes disdain the useful counsel
of Timodes, preferring to commit
all strength at once to Fate. Both dukes urge on
their men to arms. The air sounds with their din.

Book Two

Now Rumor coursed the cities of the Persians,
announcing that the Great One was advancing
with fateful vengeance for his land's past wrongs.
The fearful din assailed the ears of Darius,
who lay ensnared in luxury's dissolution.
Though he outstripped that young foe in his power—
he boasted better arms, and greater wealth
in coin and service of his vassal kings,
maturity in age, and full-grown strength—
yet had long peace and Mars' infrequent usage
suppressed the king's faint spirits. Thus he stood
inferior in all things to that duke

whom he could have excelled, if only will
to fight had matched his capabilities.
But lest his royal majesty should seem
to have less strength, as terror weighed him down,
there thundered from his mouth a haughty tirade,
and all the subject peoples came together
into encampments: through his kingdoms flew
the edict that all youths should fall to arms.
[18] Meanwhile, that Darius might not appear
to stand by idly, he dispatched a letter
to his opponent: "Darius, king of kings,
the kinsman of the gods, writes Alexander,
his servant: Spare your tender, growing years.
Though sprung from noble stock, you're still a boy:
the sapling is unsuited to the axe.
Put off the arms that you so rashly donned;
return to the embrace of your chaste mother.
I send you gifts more suited to your age:
the harness of a child, and a round ball,
and well-filled coffers to relieve the expense
of your companions, and to ease your passage.
But if your breast is vexed by so much madness
that, over peace and friendship, you would choose
the foe in battle, I'll dispatch my knights,
such servants as will lash you savagely,
consigning you to torment and death's darkness."
[34] Alexander, perturbed to some degree,
replied at once through clenched teeth to the men
who'd borne the Persian tyrant's message to him:
"We're glad that Darius is so pleasant with us;
but hear a far nobler interpretation
of your king's gifts: the round shape of the ball
nicely describes the spherical appearance
of the round earth, which I'll subdue withal.
These leather thongs I'll use upon the Persians,
when I break Darius' ancient treasure-houses."
He'd spoken, and he set in wax his image,
endowing the ambassadors with gifts.
[45] But Darius now heard through Rumor's flight

of Mennon's death, and wavered in his breast.
Yet turning the adversities of Fortune
into their contrary, he passed amidst
the princes' ranks and throngs of infantry
towards Euphrates, where whole nations waited,
flashing with gold, a broad, vast sea of peoples.
The show of force set ramparts round his heart,
and from the daybreak, till the stars appeared,
and Phoebe on the mountain ridge trailed Hesperus,
he took their count with ever-rising spirits,
according to the example set by Xerxes.
The endless phalanx left the palisade,
and passed innumerable through verdant fields:
its scattering made the numbers seem still greater.
So, too, the bleating sheep go to spring pastures:
at dawn they're counted, that the shepherd may
return as many as the pen sent out,
and zealous Baucis, anxious of the outcome,
commits them to goat-footed Faunus, lest
the wolf decrease their count by herder's negligence.
    [64] Yet earlier still, a bitter fight had raged,
the first assault of Darius on the Great One.
Beneath Duke Mennon's illustrious command,
six hundred thousand noblemen had battled.
Stronger in arms though lesser in his numbers,
Alexander routed them, and entered
the now-defeated hall of wealthy Midas.
The ancients called it Gordium; now it's Sardis.
Here twin seas hedge in Asia with the crash
of waves contending in the narrow straits.
Here the Sangarius is equidistant
from either sea, and yet its waters pour
upon the shores of each. Here in Jove's temple
the wain of Father Midas gleamed on high
with Asia's ancient, fatal yoke, and yet
with hidden cunning were the ropes entwined
and crushed together by long-passing time,
and none could find their head to loose the knots.
This was the town's sure faith, that Fate's stern order

had destined him to gain all Asia's realm
who loosed those bonds. Lust to fulfill that destiny
moved Alexander to raise up the yoke.
He struggled briefly to undo the tangle,
but saw he strove in vain; and since the omen
might strike adversely those who watched nearby,
"What matter, then, O princes," he declaimed,
"by what means or what skill Fate's silent riddles
should be laid open?" With such words, he seized
a sword and cut the knots, thus either mocking
the cast of Fortune, or perhaps fulfilling it.
[91] Dispatching troops against the Cappadocians,
he passed from there to Ancyra, whose inhabitants
he left obedient to his commands.
When morning dawned, the hastening Macedonian
in one day's time covered five hundred stades
with restless steps, rushing to overtake
the timid king: for Asia's steep approach,
the land's narrow defiles, were cause for fear,
and so he hastened to meet Darius
while still he occupied Cilicia's plains.
But eastern dew still dripped from Phoebus' lamp,
when Darius first moved from the Euphrates.
The hollow rocks echoed the clarion blasts,
the valleys answered, and the shattered air
doubled their roar, while thunder rolled the clouds.
[103] Amidst such din arising from the camps,
this was the order of the Persian troops.
On golden wheels a silver altar bore
the fire the Medes call holy and eternal.
Lines of white horses drew the carts of Jove.
Twelve nations, though diverse in dress and tongue
and custom, flanked in one well-ordered column
ten golden wagons crusted with bright gems.
About ten thousand men in gleaming wains
rode forth, whom vulgar error called Immortals,
while fifteen thousand kinsmen of the king
rode out, all clad in rich-hemmed robes like women.
Amidst them all was carried Darius

upon a car of ponderous mass, that flashed
with golden rays, around him on all sides
the gods' unnumbered effigies: barbarous luxury
and pomp of blazing gems proclaimed him king.
The bird that bears Jove's arms hung over him.
Fashioned of clay, its gilt wings blocked the heat
of burning summer, while before him marched
ten thousand spearsmen: weapons tipped with gold
gleamed silver on the whole length of their shafts.
[122] And further still, the king bade march beside him
two hundred men whom royal blood distinguished,
while thirty thousand of the finest troops
brought up the rear, lest Greeks attempt to pierce
the king's formation. Next, there came a car
filled by the Persian tyrant's mother, and
his wife and children rode nearby, surrounded
by all the appurtenances of the royal house.
Then nearly fifty courtesans were carried
in wains that groaned beneath their weight—it was
the custom, then, of Persia's duke to lead
his whole household beneath his battle standards.
Six hundred mules were laden down with coins;
three hundred hump-backed camels bore their burden.
Around this hundred-thousand-strong formation
strode many a slinger with his supple thongs.
Last came the light-armed soldiers, beyond number.
The whirling dust stirred up by feet and axles
engulfed the golden stars, and blocked their light.
[140] Meanwhile, the Macedonian advanced
towards the place that later generations
know as the Camp of Cyrus; fleeing Persians
had laid Cilicia's fields to waste before him.
He therefore sent a force under Parmenion
to save a half-dead Tarsus from their flames—
Tarsus that was adorned, as Scripture tells,
by his illustrious birth through whom faith's lamp
shone on nations long blinded by their error.
Pure and unsullied, through the city's midst
there flows the Cignus, drawing its cold streams

from bubbling springs. Content with its own waters,
receiving none from other falling torrents,
it tosses pebbles in its swirl, and sand
rolls playfully beneath its swift descent.
[153] Here for the first time, Alexander learned
that no man's safety can endure forever:
adversity is mixed with happier outcomes.
You could have seen Fate struggling with blind chance,
when luck, which favored all his undertakings,
began to fail, and dashed his army's hopes.
It was midsummer, when the sun in Leo
sets July ablaze, and fiery vapors
crack parched Cilician fields at mid-day's height.
The channel's cool and lovely guise enticed
the Macedonian, caked with sweat and dust,
to leap into the waves, before his body
had lost its heat. At once the man's whole frame
grew stiff, when plunged into the icy liquid:
the spirit found his arteries all blocked,
and left the body empty; vital warmth
was shut up by the water's chill and faltered.
His men drew forth the lifeless, stricken king,
and through the camp a wailing tumult rose.
The youth of Greece fell into lamentation:
"O Alexander, flower of youth, what power,
what chance compelled you, naked, to a death
unlooked-for among friends? O wicked Fortune,
fickle as falling leaves, harsher than tigers,
more savage than the deadly Hydra, crueler
than any monster, fearsome as Tesiphone,
why do you cut the prince's flowering years
before his day? Thus far you've nurtured him;
what drives you now to play the stepmother
to him whom all the world adopts as king?
O best of kings, what end awaits the men
who followed you far from their native land,
to which return is blocked by scorching deserts?
Shall we attack our enemies without you?

But who could worthily succeed so great a king?"
[186] Blind Fortune heard these words, while on the ground
she sat and turned her wheel with languid hand.
Revived, she rose, and smiled upon the Greeks
with a glad face, rebuked their fears, and whispered
a few words to herself: "What fatal darkness
lies on the unknowing minds of men, that they
reproach me so unjustly and so often?
All other goddesses play out their roles,
yet me alone they censure, whom they extol,
as long as I confer some benefit,
with greatest praise. I'm treated as a criminal
as soon as I withdraw my sovereign hand—
as though a stable nature could contain me.
If I remained one and the same toward all,
I'd scarcely have the proper name of Fortune.
My nature's fixed law lies in lawless motion,
and only movement makes me stable." When
she'd spoken, the king's morbid limbs revived
with fuller spirit, and began to stir,
but grave disease burned in his inward parts.
[204] Still he raised up his face with steady eye,
and said, "Shall Alexander, then, be vanquished
in his own camp, seized by the bloody victor
with Mars nowhere in sight? The foe's proximity
brooks no delay, yet plodding doctors wait
upon the crisis of the illness. Enemies
will howl barbarically, their prey denied them,
and yet the king, an ignominious exile,
will lie unlauded, stripped on hostile shores.
But if physicians' skill can mend my health,
let them attend to it, and let them know
it's time for war, not life, that I desire.
Though ailing still, if only I am able
to stand before my men, the Persian ranks
will flee headlong, while cheering Greeks pursue them."
[218] The king's reckless desire and vehemence
moved those near him to fearful hesitation,

lest hastening the cure should give the illness
occasion for increase. But Philip, whom
his father had bestowed as guardian of his health,
gave warrant to allow a three-day interval,
though all the while, he anxiously kept watch
until his health returned and illness fled.
Now from his general there came a letter
to warn the king: the doctor was corrupted
by Darius' gold and marriage to his sister.
Three times Aurora had cast her glinting flames
over a world released from shadows, when
the king, as he prepared to drain the cup,
was led to doubt his guiltless doctor's faith.
But when the draught was finished, he gave over
the writ with trembling hand, that his Archigenes
might read it. As he scanned it, in his face
no trace of shame was visible. Then he smiled
and said, "Good king, release your soul from care,
and shut out fear; allow this medicine's power
to be absorbed. He who denounces me
perhaps burns with more zeal than others, lest
you perish thus. Or else, to speak more truly,
he droops in livid jealousy of our skill;
or, bold for your destruction, he descries
the crimes of guiltless men. He who accuses
the innocent of treason is not rightly
thought innocent himself, for guilt denounces
most bitterly the guilt it finds within.
Thus sometimes wrongfully the just are bound,
and in the lying court sin goes unfound."
He bade the king's fear vanish by such words.

[245] The balm imbued his veins and inmost parts,
and caused the spent disease's seeds to perish.
Color now cheered his face, its paleness waned,
and ruddiness flowed over his white features.
His mind returned, his inner strength revived.
The princes then ran eagerly to Philip.
They threw their arms around his neck in joy,

and hailed him as his country's saving father.
When next the sun shone from the gleaming heavens,
the king rode forth upon his splendid mount
to show himself throughout the camp, and shake
slow fear from timid minds; his voice and mien
restored then to his men their wonted courage.
[257] Thereafter, when he'd crushed the nearby cities,
and paid the gods what he had earlier vowed
for restoration of his health, he set
his iron ranks against the walls of Issus.
Parmenion came forth to meet him there
and lead him in: the townsmen had all fled.
[262] The princes there deliberated whether
they should extend the lines still further, or
await the enemy where now they stood.
At length, their judgment held it advantageous
to trust their strength to Fate between the mountains,
where cliffs rose up on either side; Parmenion
deemed that the forces of both tyrants would
prove equal in the narrow gorge. But Sisenes
suffered an unjust death: it was believed
the stealthy gold of Darius had bought him,
since he'd suppressed some knowledge. And the tyrant
was not unknowing of his end's unfairness.
[272] To Darius came his Grecian mercenaries,
whose flight was spurred by exile. Into camp
they rode under the leadership of Timodes,
and offered useful counsel to the king.
They urged that he should turn his hastening wheels
upon a backward course, while time remained,
and on a path traced by his flying dust
seek out the wide and level fields once more.
But if a base retreat would shame the king,
lest his departure cast a dire portent
upon his men, he should at least divide
his treasures and his martial strength: if Fortune
should favor Argive troops in Mars' first contest
—forbid it, gods!—young men and resources

would still remain for later strife. Exposure
of all to Fortune's single blow in war
would be no little or unwillful madness.
[286] They gave him useful counsel, but it seemed
vain to the Persian princes, who intended
to lead the king astray, bidding him punish
the mercenaries with a well-earned death:
they claimed the hired Greeks wished to divide
the treasure, and so, loaded with such spoils,
to reconcile the Macedonian king
and make their peace. The king in his good will
stopped up his ears, offended by their warnings.
"Princes," he answered, "let such outrage hold
no sway within our lifetime. Shall I damn
men who have followed my encampment, men
who trusted in my faith? Such savage infamy
shall never taint my staid and waning years."
With such words and with thanks, he sent away
the Grecian mercenaries, but disdained
a king's retreat, lest he be thought a fugitive.
He burned now to join battle and to strive
among the narrow mountains, but first settled
the matter of the treasure, giving orders
to carry its chief portion to Damascus.
Yet keeping to the custom of the ancients,
his royal spouse, his sister, and his children
all sought their fate within the encampment's bounds.
[306] Thereafter, sure the strength of kings would clash
when next the Titan raised his flaming orb,
Darius climbed to a knoll that swelled above
the middle of his camp. A branching laurel
there hid sweet-smelling herbs amidst its tresses.
Beneath this copse, those who sing forest songs
recall that wanton satyrs often leered
at choruses of nymphs. Upon the left, a fountain
descends, where purple grasses cast their shadows.
The playful brook hides in spring's cloak, and waters
the inner reaches with its twisting rill;
its noisy chatter makes the mountains deaf.

Here, Flora, Mother Cybele bursts forth
and weds you to the West Wind, and the fountain
makes fecund all the valley by its grace—
just as the Rhône descends from Alpine rocks
high at its spewing source, there where Maximian
slew Eastern troops: the wave of blood augmented
the river's stream, and mingled gore burst upward
into the heavens, scorning earthen banks;
the Theban legion's death drenched all Agaunum.
[319] From here, the placid eye of Darius
gazed down on peers and commoners alike.
He summoned forth his dukes, and made division
among those who would soon march into danger.
At length he spoke; his pious lips shaped prayers
fit for his age, and by the very aspect
of his long-seasoned face he won their favor:
"Heirs of the gods, a peerless race in war,
Persians—whose nation's ancient lineage
descends from Belus, that man who first was given
the veneration of a holy idol,
and earned a starry throne among the immortals—
cast all fear from your hearts. What shameful folly
to call it a real fight, when slaves usurp
armed force against their master. Royal power
goes forth not to a war, but vengeance, when
it punishes rebellious slaves, subdues
such caitiffs, and protects its native land.
That bastard boy has seized his kingdom's governance,
imagining all things will yield to him.
Green youth's unheeding folly strikes out rashly
for every opportunity, preferring
to die in combat, rather than to yield.
But now his empty spirit, drained of hope,
grows faint, as he recalls the losses born
beside the River Granicus. In some part
he hesitates at these new-felt afflictions.
What outrage! Ragtag slaves, weak paupers, dare
to rise against the lords of all earth's wealth.
I'd like to know what fury goads you on,

poor Macedonian, by what skill you boast
you can lay claim to Cyrus' empire—Cyrus,
to whom Croesus and Lydia bent the knee,
along with every tyrant under heaven!
That king, though dead, still reigns in my succession;
in my life lives that buried monarch's fortune.
If ancient monuments remain, if memory
still knows our fathers' record, who knows not
that we trace back our lineage to the Giants?
Who has heard nothing of our strife with gods,
the bricks baked by our forebears, and the mortar
with which they built the Tower? Who forgets
the city whose eternal name derives
from tongues' confusion? Go forth, then, O princes!
Summon again your fathers' strength, and stand
for country and its noble reputation.
Let no poor upstart trample underfoot
the soil and monuments of your ancestors.
But if the hateful foe—I loathe to say it—
drive any of you from the field, and tax you
as you flee through the countryside, if king
and country and your fellow citizens
cannot command your perseverance, then
at least your wives and sons, whom hostile slaughter
will overtake here in the camp, may plead
for your return to battle. But no fear,
for Victory applauds the Persian dukes.
In sleep I watched a rain of wandering sparks
sow fire among the Macedonian tents.
Their mad duke, clad in Babylonian garb,
approached the city walls in purple splendor.
I saw him brought before me and then vanish.
I say no more, but call the sun to witness—
that never-ending light, whose golden rays
we grant their first birth in our territories—
they are my foes who loose their reins in flight."
    [372] He would have spoken more, but on swift feet
a messenger reported that the Greeks
had quit their place, and all their frightened ranks

had chosen flight: seizing on any shortcut
through forest to the sea, they now pitched down
the rocky heights upon their headlong paths.
So flattery enticed the prince's ear.
Vain joy brought hesitation, but then scorn
of more delay. The army crossed the river
and sought a hurried road through stony wastes
to overtake the royal fugitive.

[381] Doomed band, where are you rushing? Do you think
this youth will flee unconquered, who considers
no crime so shameful as retreat, who fears
only one thing, that sluggards should escape?
If he were given such a choice, to conquer
by means of flight, or to succumb to fugitives
and yet in his defeat resist the foe,
he'd hesitate which course held less dishonor.

[388] Now swiftly the Chaldean ranks neared Issus,
and watchmen saw them coming. Flashing gold
and gems gleamed from their armored ranks; the sun
was covered by the whirling dust they stirred.
A zealous guardsman ran from the high citadel
to tell the Greeks the Babylonian tyrant
approached with every race of humankind.
He whom only surcease of warfare troubled
could scarce believe the joyous news. Among
his companies, he led the way and thundered,
"To arms, to arms, O men of Greece!" The first
to leave the city, he crashed against the Persians;
thereafter followed young men clad in armor.
So hungry-jawed Lycaon rushes down
upon his prey, when, hanging from dry teats,
his whining cubs implore his help, and famine,
conceived in empty caverns, foments slaughter—
at last his hunger drives him out into
the open fields: the sheep freeze in astonishment,
not daring flight and other maws that wait
within the woods; the shepherd frees the dogs,
and goads them from the hill with staff and voice.
No otherwise, the Macedonian king

raged wantonly against those savages,
who just now had supposed he'd fled in terror.
[408] The parted ranks of the opposing line
beheld their sudden coming forth to war,
and feared hope had deceived them. On they rushed
despite dismay, but shouts and speed of rushing troops
and turmoil in the ranks scattered their forces:
they were prepared more for a march, than battle
against a foe. Yet Darius again
drew up the ranks, wisely deliberating
to ring the foe on all sides with vast forces—
a useful plan, and much to his advantage
in its devising, but that shameless Fortune
wields power beyond reason: she alone
maintains safe circumstances, lightens burdens,
voids mankind's plans and breaks their solemn compacts,
weakens what's strong, moves mountains, shatters peaks.
[422] The Macedonian ranks still kept their order
and held their set formations on the slopes.
The king deployed a phalanx of the infantry
against the Persians at the forefront. On
the right flank stood Parmenion's son, Nicanor,
and with him Ptolemy, Amyntas, Perdicas,
Meleager, Coenos, Clitus, each in charge
of his own column. But to you, Parmenion,
second to none in war, the left flank was
entrusted. Swift Craterus followed, and
with him Antigonus, and fierce Philotas.
Exposed before the enemy, outstripping
the banners of his host, driving his steed
upon the right, the Macedonian
flashed out, his spear and sword and flaming helmet
all bringing terror of his might at arms.
Hephaestion clung closest to his side,
the sharer of his secrets, like the king
in zeal and age, but lovelier of form.
[439] Riding before the banners of his soldiers,
he pressed the generals with glad entreaties,
gave praise, strengthened the hesitant, increased

the courage of the daring, checked the errant,
and drew the wings back in when they were scattered.
Enticing slaves with hopes of liberty,
the poor and greedy with reward, he prodded
those who marched too slowly with his spear.
Now he rode 'round this group of men or that,
now bade them stretch the bow, now cast their slings
if hostile troops stood far away, now fight
with sword and axe if foes were near at hand;
and when they slowed their pace, harangued them thus:
"Scions of Mars, the whole world longs to feel
your laws' force, and to lie beneath your sway.
Behold the awaited day, on which wise Fortune
prepares to grant the triumph often promised,
whose foretaste I perceived in Europe, when
you laid to waste Thebes' race and her foundations,
and conquered Athens by sheer terror only.
Behold the weakling throngs flashing with gold,
behold how gems gleam in their womanish ranks:
they offer more of booty than of danger.
Gold's to be won with iron. Lisping catamites
know how to threaten, but shun swords and wounds.
They'll seek the paths of flight through rocks and forests,
when once the lethal sword point finds their entrails,
and enemy blood is spattered on the fields.
Dull, broken swords will prove regard for me,
when I see shields crushed under myriad blows.
Your right hand's savagery will show the love
your minds profess; your breasts hold Alexander
only so dear as your blades can make plain.
Conquer once more those conquered once before.
Who spares the sword against the enemy
is enemy to himself; who grants him life
denies his own. War knows no clemency
in piety toward the foe. The hand that spares
is harsh against itself, and should be severed.
The sluggish fear to meet their death by chance,
and so dare not to go and face it squarely.
Before your minds set all the injurious slaughter

inflicted on the Greeks by Persian dukes!
Do you suppose the sons make restitution
for all their fathers' deeds? That whole huge nation
would not suffice to pay the penalty.
I'll pay back Europe's rout with Asia's ruin.
Persia will expiate the crimes of Xerxes
in Darius' defeat. Bear forth the banners
where I am leading; strike the palisade,
advance among their serried ranks with slaughter.
Divide the battle with me, not its plunder:
let booty go to those who follow me;
glory alone suffices as my share.
I claim the title; take yourselves the wealth."
He'd spoken, and the front lines crashed together.
The Persians loosed their shouts in horrid wails,
and trumpets filled the plains with fearful braying.
On every side there rose a din, and clarions
struck at the sky, the mountain tops sang back
the raucous chant, and disembodied Echo
could never answer with so many voices.
[494] But Darius' arms flashed forth, the toil of smiths,
bearing remembrance of the men of old.
A shield of molten circles sevenfold
made contest of the sun's unvanquished face.
Here shone the origins of Darius' sires,
and all the profane ranks of Giant race.
The earthborn brothers you might there behold
sitting beneath Nimrod, their prince, upon
the plain of Shinar: there, once flood-borne death
receded, rose the tower of burnt brick,
and there a single earlier human tongue
was variously—wondrous to tell—divided.
Elsewhere, Chaldea's king assays a march
towards the Holy City. Glorious battles
and victories over Hebrew foes gleam forth.
A captive tribe follows the victor's car
with downcast gaze. The walls and Temple lie
leveled to the bare soil. Stripped of his sight
as of his throne, the despot is borne off

within the ramparts of the enemy town.
[511] Yet, lest the faults of some obscure the praise
of ancient kings, the sculptor's right hand spurns
long stories it was seemly to omit.
Among so many worthy martial deeds
and kingly triumphs, it was shame to grave
a king sustained by pasture and by stream,
who bellowed in a guise transformed by sin.
He passes over, too, the father turned
back to his former image and sound mind,
whose savage son, it's claimed, disgrace to tell,
lest he should never rule the realm alone,
carved up his sire at Joachim's advice,
and in a trackless waste scattered the limbs,
a feast for vultures.
[522] The noble Persian realm begins upon
the shield's last part. On this you may behold
Belshazzar drinking from the sacred gold, and spy
a hand that writes of changing destinies,
whose hidden riddle Daniel solves. Around
the whole shield's circuit, at its outer edges
the narrative of Cyrus runs: here Lydia
is glad to be subdued by such a prince;
it was Croesus that a sly Apollo tricked.
Yet Tamiris dared try the rush of war,
opposed force with her own, beat back in battle
the unbroken one, and by unlucky stars
pressed down that head adorned with so much praise.
Imperial glory, lo! How you deceive!
How many snares engross the human lot!
The mighty Cyrus, darling of the world,
its ruler both on land and sea, whom virtue
had raised up to the pinnacle of things,
whom fame ensconced among the gleaming stars,
sole master of himself by his own strength,
the one and only hammer of the world,
was broken by a lady soft in war.
[540] You mortals, curb the pride by which you raise
your spirits and with heaped-up wealth despise

your lessers. Cease, you conquerors, to live
ungrateful to the highest Conqueror.
He who was able to bestow the crown
and sceptre, strength, and wealth, and victory
retains the power to remove them all.

Book Three

The Headings of the Third Book

The third book sings of arms and dying nations.
The Persians fall, and Darius' household treasures
are plundered. Sister, mother, wife, and son
of seven years are captured. Sidon falls,
and Tyre is wholly razed. Amidst great peril
Gaza's taken. A few seek Libyan Ammon.
His strength renewed, the Persian king again
rushes to arms. The failure of the moon
breeds treason in the Macedonian camp.
The seers, consulted, speak of adverse Fortune.

Book Three

Now din of arms and war's fierce slaughter conquered
the blare of trumpets. Arrows veiled the stars,
and javelins in thickened clouds obscured
the upper air. Foremost against the Persians,
more swiftly than a catapulted stone,
the Macedonian thrust his spear point forward.
He turned his mount where gold flashed from the shields
of kings set side by side, where plenteous gems
shone proudly upon helmets; where the shape
of Darius' flaming dragon burned with terror,
and sucked the winds into its golden jaws.
    [11] As he sought out one fit for his first blows,

Arethas, Syria's prefect, came before him,
upon whose gilded spear a lion blew:
pendant and waving, it rivaled heaven's stars,
while on his war-cap blazed a carbuncle.
First with a trembling thrust the Chaldean pierced
through Alexander's shield. But with a rattle
the ashen beam shrank from the narrow opening,
and shattered dryly. Valiantly advancing,
Pellaeus split the boss, where barbarous gold
shone bright upon the prince Arethas' shield;
yet still unsatisfied, he rent the weave
of the three-layered mail-coat, and his spear
roamed deadly through that heart, and drank its spirit.
Stricken, he fell, and from the gaping wound
gore rushed to stain the ground a purple hue.
The Grecian phalanx with a mighty shout
declared their king had conquered, and had claimed
the war's first fruits. They deemed the omen lucky,
and bore a joyous uproar to the stars.
[28] The ranks closed up. Illustrious in arms,
Clitus and Ptolemy rushed toward the foe,
as swiftly as two lions' rage impels them,
when famished hunger drives them at twin bulls,
and the lashing of their tails abets their fury.
Here Ptolemy lays low a Parthian,
Dodontes, whom he pierces through the temples,
and leaves him moaning as his brains pour out.
But Clitus tries to topple Arthophilus,
and in their turn they trade blows, till their lances
are both bent blunt and skid across their shields.
They're matched arm's strength for strength, and steed for steed,
their breastplates, shields, and corselets all are even,
helm dashes against helm. Both mounts and riders
straightway collapse on buckled knees; they lie
exhausted and near lifeless for some time.
But when their bodies' strength returns, Clitus
is first to move upright upon his feet,
and with his sword, as Arthophilus struggles
to rise up, mows his head with one fierce stroke,

and leaves him to the earth, in need of burial.
Mazaeus, known for beauty, speech, and prowess,
laid low Iollas on the Greeks' left flank.
Philotas stood nearby with ready vengeance;
but since Mazaeus fled upon his horse,
he rushed to challenge Ochus at close range,
and with his drawn sword's edge slashed through his flank.
[53] Hyrcanian knights meanwhile hedged in Philotas
amidst his toil of bloodshed; through their ranks
burst swift Antigonus, Coenus, Craterus,
and Parmenion himself, without whose aid
no deed worthy of song would be ascribed
to Alexander. (But I judge it better
to pass over in silence what reward
he garnered for his merits.) Mida lay
on Coenus' spearpoint, and Antigonus
slew Phylax with his blade. Craterus faced
Amphilochus, and, shattering his helmet,
he pulled him lifeless from his chariot;
the Persian's driver joined him in his fall,
now dragging ruptured entrails in the dust.
[63] Parmenion, marked for an unjust fate,
rushed in his wonted manner on the Persians.
King-born Isannes and bold Dinus struck
his flank with spears. Yet he remained unshaken,
advancing to Horestes' aid, who fled
on trembling feet over the jagged rocks.
No sooner had he spied him, but he cast
Isannes from his horse, pierced through the breast:
the fleeing knight was thus restored to arms.
His steed's hoof trampled Dinus, as he stood
with sword grasped in his hand, and left him crippled.
To these he joined Elas and Agilon
and Arabic Cherippus.
Now by spear
and now by javelin's cast, Eumenidus
savaged the Persians on another front.
His blade laid waste Diaspes, and he dyed
his spear red in Eudochius' lung. He clove

the bones of men, and trampled crowds of chieftains.
No less, upon the right flank, did Nicanor
asperge the fields with gore, and soak the plain
in slaughter as he fought. Eclimus faced him,
a youth of beauty, richer still in birth,
who drew his lineage from Cyrus' blood.
His blows raged on Nicanor's shield, just as
the flying hail of early spring will pound
against the roofing tiles, but still the house
in safety scorns the anger of the air.
With hardened heart, Nicanor rushed to claim
the outrage of that piteous carnage, smiting
the lad where the bright mail-coat opened up
to leave his eyes a window. With his spear
he put out both those lights: the ashen shaft
upon its path of crime ran through the one,
and then deprived him of the other's use.
    [90] Amidst dire danger on the opposing front
stood Prince Negusar, Ninus' famous scion,
a Ninevite whose skillfully plied axe
swung to and fro against those in his path;
his skill indeed assailed the very Fates
with darts hurled from behind.
He raged now with his blade, now with his javelin,
now brains lay savaged by his two-edged sword.
His shaft ran through Elis, the son of Actor,
and Dorilus was widowed of his arm
by the broad sword. He slew Hermogenes:
the axe sliced through his neck. But when Philotas
beheld him wasting Greeks with varied carnage,
he swiftly drew his blade, and flew to where
the bronze upon his helmet's crown shot light.
He struck the cap; its smoothness scorned the blow.
Yet not without its toll the edge descended:
it cut away the left hand where he held it
before his brow. Lo! now the right prepared
to avenge her sister, confident of slaughter
though vulnerable herself, raising the axe

and threatening the foe with its next fall.
Perchance Philotas might have mourned his spirit
snatched early from him; but Amyntas rode
to his assistance, thrusting his shield forward,
so that the dreadful engine's blow pierced it,
but stuck within the boss. Negusar burned
to draw it out, but his attacker's sword
made strangers of his arm and shoulder, where
the ulna is connected. For a time,
the pain aroused his strength; seeing his body
made useless by his hands' loss, he performed
the only deed he could: upon his horse
he hurled himself towards Iollas, and
all three together fell. Iollas perished,
run through with spears, and with him, too, his mount.
But harsh Negusar, neither were you spared
by clouds of missiles, nor by such a ruin.

[119] The sodden turf lay hidden by the corpses
that now concealed the earth, fields were awash
in swamps of gore, valleys were filled with blood.
Each side sustained great carnage, but the slaughter
of Medes made drunker still the fields. Though countless,
the barbarous foe was thinned, and failed in spirit,
nor did the smaller Macedonian band
cease striking—fervent zeal made up their numbers.
Like lightning Alexander pressed upon them
amidst their flight, and through the trackless spaces,
through swords and throngs of knights, he picked his way
toward Darius. But Oxatreus, closest
in birth to Darius, pulled in the column.
Here grief and moans arose. Youths of keen spirit
perished on either side, and death enfolded
the leaders of both parties in a whirlwind.
Bellona scattered from her gory hands
death's every guise upon the Persians: here
one groans through his slashed throat, another lies
pierced through the bowels with iron. Here a stake
has brained one man, the sling or bow slays others.

One vomits bloody slime—his neck is broken;
another's guts fall out, swords claim a third.
Some tremble, dying; some lie still and dead.
[140] Now Zoroas of Memphis stood before him,
girded with precious arms, whom none surpassed
in starry lore, or in foreknowledge of
mundane affairs. He knew beneath what star
the fields suffer a dearth, what year bears fruit,
the source from which come winter's snows, what mildness
impregnates the warm soil in early spring,
why summer burns, what grants autumn a robe
hung round with grapes. He knew whether the circle
can be squared, whether music forms
celestial harmonies, and what proportion holds
among four elements; what force compels
the planets on a course against the world,
what grades divide them, and which star impedes
the rage of the adverse Old Man, which renders
him more propitious, and which tempers Mars;
how each seeks out its house, which holds its sway
within this hemisphere. He sought their paths,
noted their hours, and all human events
perceived among the stars. I say too little—
all heaven's vault he held within his breast.
And since he presaged fate and coming death
by heaven's portents, nor could turn aside
the fatal sequence, boldly he pushed through
to meet the Macedonians' commander.
Demanding slaughter at the great man's hands,
hating his very life with savage force,
he ran to meet him at the raging front,
in labor with his own death. From his car
he pressed the prince's shield with darts like hailstones,
and added shouted insults to his spears:
"Whelp of Nectanabus, and endless shame
of your own mother (who'd deny it?), why
do you waste blows upon some wretch? Now turn
your rage against me, if you still possess

your strength. Strike now instead at me, whose prowess
is shielded by the ark of sevenfold wisdom,
that you may claim a double victory."
 [173] Astonished, Alexander pitied him
in his desire to die, and peaceably
addressed him: "Portent that you are, live on,
whoever you may be. Do not destroy
in death, I pray, the lodging of such arts.
O never may my right hand and my sword
endeavor to make gory such a brain.
The world has use of you. What error, then,
drives you in longing toward the Stygian banks,
where knowledge never flowers?" So he'd spoken.
But Zoroas dismounted, drew his sword,
and gashed his thigh where mail-coat leaves the greave,
christening thus the battlefield with blood.
The Macedonian roared, and yet loosed rein,
driving his horse away to spare the other.
Thus, far removed, he checked his fury. But
Meleager rushed up and struck Zoroas,
cutting away both knees, where calf meets thigh.
A varied rabble then hacked him to pieces,
and set the man again among the stars.
 [189] But then on Darius fell all the weight
of present danger. What was he to do?
He saw the fields thick with his soldiers' blood,
saw all around him lifeless corpses of
so many nobles; there his charioteer
lay with a broken neck amidst the horses,
whose guts were strewn behind them. While he wavered
between escape on foot or suicide,
Perdicas cast his javelin: his head
received the blow, and yet the skull protected
the brain within. Then Darius was hurled
from his high chariot, and would no more
endure the armed ranks' crush. On foot he turned,
and sought the forest's shortened paths among
the base and fleeing, till a borrowed steed

had borne him over great Euphrates, and
he'd taken shelter in high Babylon.
[203] But then Mazaeus and the others, whose
preeminence of conquering valor still
permitted them no flight from raging Mars,
knew that the secret course of Darius
had saved him from the deadly wrack of war.
At once, their daring, routed by such ills,
left off its great endeavors and served fear:
their loyalty was turned to cringing. Now
the mob of dukes drew up their ranks in flight,
for when the head had wavered, of necessity
the limbs were shaken; parts failed where the sum
was moved. The host was cut down from behind;
another slaughter raged. Their flight but gained them
calamitous disgrace and death, when honorably
they could have died for lord and fatherland.
[215] And now the glutted sword returned to scabbard:
the Greeks, victorious, at the victor's order
paused in the slaughter, rushing toward the treasure
that waited, opulent and lying deep
within the grove, as booty to be plundered.
Swiftly the victor moved to dole the wealth
in equal shares. They loaded it on horses,
and greedy axles groaned beneath the weight.
The satchel's stuffed now, vomiting out gold:
its top is split, one more coin it can't hold.
It scorns a knot, refusing to be tied.
The hand, though wearied, still unsatisfied,
continues to reach out; the soldier's boot
and ample pouch must swell to hold the loot.
[225] The next assault then fell upon the women,
whose numbers stood defenseless. Necklaces
were ripped from marble shoulders, torques were seized,
ears lost their ornaments—and brides now felt
unwelcome arms; virginity endured
raw force. A bloodstained hand gropes private parts
and lays its bed of lust in open air.
Some feel defilement's stain, while others grieve

and so receive a pardon, since main force
alleviates the sufferer's guilt: coercion
diminishes the blame. But Darius' house,
his mother and his royal sister-consort,
their son and all their train, were saved such shame,
their majesty preserved. In golden cars
they rode into the Grecian camp. Such was
the conquering Alexander's clemency.
In Darius' mother he beheld his own,
and granted his foe's wife the name of sister.
In mercy he adopted as his son
the boy of seven years: such love of virtue
still reigned then in his breast.
(Had he endured
in that same disposition, infamy
had never known the means to denigrate
a reputation splendid in its honors;
but when the royal pleasures of the Persians
fell in his grasp and drew him to their ways,
and opulence, the mother of excess,
convinced him all was lawful, Fortune spoiled
his prior nature. So that earlier wave
was pushed back, crashing on the rocks of vice.
His earlier piety towards his foes
gave way to murderous hatred of his friends;
he turned at last to war within his house,
and judged nothing unlawful to a tyrant.
And who must not confess that he affected
high Jove as his own father? He commanded
men's faith that Jove had sired him; he believed
his power had surpassed all humankind.
A man, he shunned humanity; it seemed
a trifle to stand highest among mortals.)
[258] Meanwhile, Parmenion was sent with troops
to take Damascus and wrest from the conquered
the treasure's remnants hidden in the city;
but there the prefect had already deemed
that all its riches must fall to the victor.
A faithless traitor to his former lord,

transformed indeed by Fortune's transient course,
he dragged his men out from the town, betraying
them to the foe. Thus by the single crime
of that one man, so many Persians fell—
and he himself with all the rest: that fate
was Darius' one solace in his grief
and many losses, when a messenger
reported that the crime's own architect
had perished for his pains amidst the vanguard.
No further did he rail at unjust Fortune,
who with an equal balance pays the guilty
—sometimes—as base deceit has merited.
Such was his balm in trouble; so most ills,
despite their setbacks, bring a kind of relish.

[274] The seventh day had raised the lamp of Phoebus
to drive the stars back from the kindled world;
the wonted obsequies of burial
had been paid out, when Alexander faced
Phoenicia's race and Sidon's ancient walls,
which he left subject to his laws. He turned
his course to Tyre, where he rejoiced to find
its men at watch upon the heights, and ready
for every martial contest. Towers stood
disposed in long array upon the walls,
a prominent defense that could stand up
to well-flung stones: wherever rocks assailed
an entrance, yeomen joined their shields, repelling
those missiles. Many a thrower plied the sling,
and catapults rained death on those below.

[288] At last the long day broke the afflicted city,
now by attack from sea, now overland,
and on both sides the engines of the Greeks
pressed on the hostile walls, from where the ships
lay at the ramparts; without much distinction
of age or sex, the victims perished, and
the sword held back from no one, doling outrage
with even justice. For he'd not yet ringed
the walls in siege, when they'd condemned to death
the soldiers sent as legates from the king

to offer peace in season of distress—
a violation of the truce they'd set.
An object therefore of the tyrant's hatred,
they merited no pardon, among whom
the embassy had found no peace or pardon.
The Macedonian gave swift command
to plunge them all in carnage, save for those
the temples shielded. Noise and lamentation
and tearful groans arose on every side;
the screams of women grazed the golden stars.
Then while the greatest turmoil surged around them,
they laid a fire where winds most pressed the city.
The famished flame now flew up to the gables,
and where the fire grew hungry, higher floors
afforded it more food and nourishment.
Lords perished with the rabble in one death,
and yet their agonies wore varied guise:
one man, fearing the blaze, ran onto swords;
another, fleeing swords, plunged in the flames;
some fled from one death to another, falling
beyond the ruined city's crumbling ramparts
into the surging currents of the deep.
Still others sought out hidden lairs in houses
now empty, where they fixed their throats in nooses
and fashioned their own death, lest they should perish
by Greek-inflicted death. Shame held back some
from seeking to evade the rush of battle:
they chose to die defending liberty,
their city's rights and laws, before the face
of their own land. That was an honorable death,
a fall unfouled, unyielding in the slaughter,
slaying and being slain with no mean vengeance.
Advancing, bound for murder, they presented
new fodder for the smiters. Smiting, smitten,
prepared for either role, they suffered death,
nor did the spouse of Venus bring less bloodshed.

[330] That noble Tyre first founded by Agenor
was thus reduced to ash. If fame bears credence,
if poets' gleaming words deserve belief,

she first learned and first taught the signs for speech,
the figures of all things. So then, unchecked,
the Macedonians' fury tamed that city
untamed through all the years. But holy peace
and true faith in the Christ of Christs restored
the ramparts of that town, where now a populace
of orthodox belief, which blazes with
the incense of the mind, adores the Name
of Him who hung upon the Cross—just as
He holds forever by paternal right
the other cities of earth's seven climes.

[342] The overthrow of Tyre might well have served
to warn the northern world's remaining nations
not to provoke the name of Macedonia
or the Pellaean's might. Yet Gaza clung
to Darius and to her first allegiance:
she rashly strove to shut out from her walls
the equal of the gods, as though perchance
mere faith could overturn the will of Fortune.
While Mars dispatched his work on either side,
raging with bloody slaughter and dire loss,
there came before the king, like one who'd fled,
a savage hiding steel beneath his shield,
who with his blade sought Alexander's head.
And yet, because the Fates' unswerving sequence
prevails unmoved, and checks the deeds of men,
the drunkard's hand swerved wide. Thus did Lachesis
prevent the man from perishing by the sword
for whom the goddess had laid up a venom
concocted long ago of Lethe's dregs—
she'd set it, ten years hence, before the duke
in its glass vessel, relying on the favor
of his own men. But since the Arab's hand
had erred in such a way, the king commanded
it be cut off with that same treacherous blade
it had so poorly wielded. Warlike fury
now woke again from earlier slumber, and
the anger of a burning heart grew raw
at the fresh treachery. While in his rage

he pressed the foe, a heavy rock struck hard
the middle of his shin; bent on its crime,
an ashen shaft grazed his left shoulder. But
despite his double wound, the Macedonian
would not leave off his bitter undertaking.
He clove the ranks, lavish of his breath,
and slew the master of the city, entering
the walls now given over by the vanquished.
[370] After the princes had disposed the kingdom
according to their judgment, thence he turned
toward Egypt. Leaving it beneath his sway,
the king burned to behold the Libyan shrine
of Ammon. Grueling the approach, intolerable
that journey, even to the few brave men
who suffered it! The parched earth longed for dew,
the sky pleaded for water, endless heat
withered the region, sterile sand lay dead;
and when its grains received the sun and wind,
and swirled more wildly under striking feet,
here, too, the Syrtes had their storms; here, too,
another Scylla bayed on a dry sea;
here lay dusty Charybdis. One man vomited
a powdery mass; sand covered yet another.
Perhaps they would have suffered lighter gales
on Neptune's sea, than on that dusty main.
Nowhere did tilled things flourish; tracks of men
were nowhere to be seen; nowhere did earth,
nowhere did tree appear before the eye.
[386] Now Dawn had four times raised her dewy chariot,
and shed her tears before the tomb of Memnon,
when Macedonia's helmsman, and the rest
of the surviving band, approached the grove
of Ammon, where they drank the fountain's waters.
Among things worthy of commemoration,
it is not fit to pass that spring in silence:
the rill meanders with a tepid course,
such time as Phoebus curbs his horses; colder
than ice it flows, when Titan burns the fields
with mid-day heat. Beneath the western course,

when welcoming Thetis cleanses out the mangers,
preparing for the horses of the Sun—
she strews ambrosia and removes their bits—
Jove's fountain warms a little from that coldness.
But when Sleep showers the world from dripping wings,
it burns more hotly than Phoebus at noon;
the more Apollo hastens to his rising,
the more the current calls to mind its mildness,
its potent fervor forced now to abate,
till growing calm again at Phoebus' dawning.
[404] The king, when he had made his consultation
of high Jove's oracle, and paid his offerings,
returned to Memphis. Indeed, he was inclined
to visit Ethiopia's scorched peoples
and Memnon's hostile fields, Aurora's throne,
the trackless places of the sun; but harsh
and unassailable remains Mars' season.
The predetermined day now stood at hand
that would behold the fight's tumultuous carnage
prepared him by the foe. More pressing tasks
hedged in the ruler's closely straitened mind.
[413] Meanwhile, the world convened in oaths of battle
as Darius regained his strength: the shame
of what had gone before, the goad of hope
in future outcomes, called him back to arms.
In the encampment knights and farmers mingled.
Fields cloaked in brambles and the root-filled earth
bemoaned their tillers' absence. Oxen strained
at wagons. Barbarous races pressed the backs
of camels, and the elephants, weighed down
with warfare's engines, walked in turreted columns,
followed by the buffalo. Advancing
upon the Argives, Xerxes never drank
the rivers dry with such a host of men,
nor did adultery's avenger gather
so many tribes at Aulis, when the deep
was insufficient for the fleet, and, at
the bidding of foul Calchas, virgin slaughter
atoned for crime, and loosed the winds in blood.

The Macedonian marveled that, though thousands
had been reduced to nothing, yet more nations
were born again for death and called to war.
No otherwise, Jove's son stood in amazement
on Libya's sands, to see Antaeus rise
once more in greater might after each fall,
until he seized him, crying, "Here you'll fall,
Antaeus; hope is vanity!" No otherwise
did Hercules, at such a cost of slaughter
among his men, subdue the fecund Hydra.
[436] Forgetful of the dangers, in despite
of all their numbers, over the Euphrates
that conqueror of lands drove on his ranks,
only to find scorched towns and smoldering fields
wherever he approached. Mazaeus had burned them
at Darius' command, that such a turn
of Fortune might bend back their course, compelling
the hungry Greeks to cease their bold endeavor
by failure of supplies. (Perhaps a path
that lay through blazing rocks might make them flee,
when they beheld all things consumed: the fields
stripped of their grain, broad places filled with fire,
where furrows begged for respite, and where Ceres,
reduced to ash, denied all sustenance.)
But Alexander seized his luck, aspiring
as always to the pinnacle of honor:
he crossed the Tigris' waters, swifter than
that stream itself, whose tigerish force imparts
its name—the Tigris, in whose surge are rolled
huge stones, before it passes savagely
into the marble waves of the great sea.
[454] Immediately, lest Darius should gain
the inner reaches of his realm, he stalked him
in such a way as when a hunting dog
tracks Actaeon along a forest ridge,
sure of his scent, or when a Gallic hunter
pursues a boar with angry iron spear.
He pitched his camp near Arbela; for now
in those same parts, he too had pitched his tents

whose death by treachery of his own men
would give that place a name of lasting infamy.
[463] It was the hour whose doubtful light bears neither
the name of day nor night, but touches each
with scant distinction, and so in its vagueness
was called dusk by the Greeks. Now Hesperus
had hastened to his dewy rising; now
the stars prepared to fill the bright sun's office,
as darkness loomed before the eyes of mortals,
while through their midst the moon passed. But Phoebe,
whose nascent course makes glad the climes of men,
grew pale just as her brother's flight revealed her.
She suffered first her wonted splendor's loss,
and then was filled with redness, like dark blood
that fouled her light. Among the Grecian ranks,
both commoners and nobles stood in terror,
since now before them rose the appointed day,
lethal for either side, when foes would rage
upon the field of war's unwelcome deity.
In heaven they beheld the lowering stars
shrink from such outrage as their signs portended.
No wonder, then, that spirits wavered, and
the hand that carried arms threatened to fall.
Hearts trembled, struck by mounting fear; the camp
was torn by raucous murmurs. Alexander
now stood accused: a treasonous rank and file
laid blame upon him, that against their will
their king compelled them to the world's far edge.
They made complaint against the trackless mountains,
lands inhospitable with Vulcan's rage,
against cities and rivers that refused
to welcome violent men. The gods opposed
their will to play the lords of humankind;
the offended stars refused their usual light,
and now their king passed man's appointed limits,
laid claim to heaven, and despised the seats
of his own native land. For one man's praise
they all endured so many dangers, gambling
on Fortune's vast reversals—now the rabble

broke forth in such complaints, and now sedition
began to flow. In full alarm, the king
summoned his council, and enjoined the seers,
whose knowledge of the stars, divinely granted,
bestows their name in all its potent craft:
what force had tinged the circle of the moon,
what had the gods decreed? He bade them speak
the fatal riddles' true significance.

[501] Among the seers and watchers of the stars
stood Aristander, shrunken with dry age.
"Leave off," he said, "your vain complaints against
the Fates: they rule the stars, and in unshaken order
preserve the courses, stations, movements, portents
the Sower of all things gave at their origin,
nor can they change one whit that deep Mind's will.
Whatever from eternity It glimpsed
of things to come—whether the sea assails
the land with whirling force; whether the earth
engulfs whole cities in its shifting flanks;
whether the fetid air emits contagion;
whether that Mind desires to cloak the day
in shadow and obscure the moon's bright horns,
or set swift Mercury on slower course—
all things descend from that high Magistrate,
apart from Whose decree the stars do nothing.
So is it when the ghastly circle of the moon
grows pale and disappears from human sight,
or when the splendor of Diana's brother
oppresses her, just as a blazing furnace
obscures a kindled lamp's weak flame in envy.
Yet, following the venerable lore
of ancient Memphis' fathers, I would say
with little doubt, the sun stands for the Greeks,
the moon for Persia; by the sun's demise
the fall of Greeks is indicated, by
that of the moon, the ruin of the Persians."

[526] So speaking, by examples he considered
the witness of the Persian leaders' deeds,
upon whom Fortune had pressed with her lash

while mournful Cynthia's horns had palely faded.
The argument of venerable old age
thus stood approved; the judgment of the seer
won their belief, and superstition, rising
amidst the rabble's trembling hearts, prevailed—
for nothing bends a crowd with greater sureness,
or puts a stronger rein to voice and hand.
When, savage, fickle, powerful, the crowd
seethes with the surging of a wandering mind,
it heeds the seers' commands and scorns the bridle
of kings, once it is moved by vain religion.
So while their sluggish minds were raised by hope
and trust in fate, while hearts were still aglow,
the Macedonian saw fit to act,
lest such hot force grow cold. Immediately,
around midnight, he bade his men strike camp,
and went before the shouting throngs, content
to ride among a vanguard of small numbers.

Book Four

The Headings of the Fourth Book

The fourth book turns the Great One to sad rites
for Darius' wife. Laments and false suspicion
vex Darius. The legates bring him answer.
On either side, formations stand prepared
for combat. Alexander fears war's image,
and calls a council. Spurning his men's answers,
he puts off sleep until the daylight hours.
Aroused from sleep, he swiftly dons his arms,
and fortifies his men by word and deed.
The lines collide, the din assails the stars.

Book Four

His countenance besmeared with pitchy smoke,
the lurid Day-star rode out a fourth time
on breathless mount before the deadly tumult.
Between the sandy whirlpool's nearby stream
and woods whose highest peaks were swathed in cloud,
the Grecian phalanx marched through verdant fields.
Driven by hope, it trod victoriously
a route the yielding enemy had left it.
Then Darius' royal spouse fell down to death
among the captive women's powerless throng:
grief for his absence, for her land's subjection,
and endless travel on the toilsome road

made sure her passing. But the conqueror—
that mightiest and most devout of kings—
felt grief no otherwise than if he'd heard
of his own mother's and his sisters' death.
The youth brought forth such tears of lamentation
as Darius might have shed. Now white old age
came to the place of death, and pious grace,
forever rare in tyrants, broke the hardness
of an unvanquished prince, who though a foe
paid tears as tribute. Only once he'd glimpsed her
after her capture; from her sumptuous mien
he drew no cause for frenzy, wishing rather
to stand as guardian of her honor and
appearance—glory fell to him more richly
in shaming neither, than in violating both.
[24] Escaping from amidst the Grecian ranks,
the eunuch Tiriotes brought the news
to Darius, who saw his clothing rent
with bloody nails, his tangled hair lying
upon his face, his visage drenched in tears.
"Whatever welfare still remains to me,"
the king said, "spoil it now, and change my fear
to mourning. I have learned unhappiness,
and know how to be buffetted by ills.
The wretched have this solace only, and
this cure for pain: they know their lot in life.
You bring news of my family's mockery,
cruel torments worse for them than any lash—
and yet I fear to say it." Then replied
the other: "Every honor and respect
that could be paid to royal ladies has
been paid to yours. But—this I dread to tell—
your noble consort, both your wife and sister,
has passed and left behind her lifeless body."
Then you might have seen the whole encampment
reduced to groans and weeping. The old man
lay lifeless, fouling in the dust his white
and noble locks: he privately supposed
his wife was slain in chaste refusal of

some outrage. Then he shut out all the others,
keeping with him only the eunuch, who
swore that the queen had borne no loss of honor,
that at the captor's hand the captive paid
no shameful price: she had received the tears
due from a husband, and a worthy bier.
But now suspicion, mingled with his grief,
pierced his loving mind, and in his frenzy
he guessed some passion sprang, as crime is wont,
between captive and captor: "In both flesh
and blood," he said, "this prisoner was noble;
her master, still a youth." What might have been
he reckoned as her will, and with such cares
his sick mind seethed, until the slave bore witness,
upon the household gods and those above,
that Darius' spouse was chaste in life and death.
Then raising up his palms and tear-drenched visage
towards the stars, thus spoke the king: "Great father
of gods, and single power over all;
ancestral deities by whose consent
the Persian empire stands, first this I plead—
make firm our kingdom; but if you have determined
that I should lose it, if Fate's puissant will
commands it to be transferred from my grasp,
let such a pious enemy as this,
so kind a conqueror, receive the realm
of Asia after me." He'd spoken, and
beseeched the gods above with flowing tears
that Fate should follow as he'd voiced his prayer.

[68] And though he'd sought peace twice before in vain,
though now his counsels were all turned toward war,
subdued by love's example in his foe,
he ordered that ten captains of the knights
should go on embassy of peace, safe under
Athena's olive branch. In eloquence
as by his age, Achillas was the foremost
among them all, and thus he now began:
"Kindest of kings, no force requires Darius
so often to seek peace of you, but rather

your own great piety, so often shown
towards our kin, demands it of him. Nor
do we regard his children and his mother
as captives, but as loved ones merely absent.
For those who still survive, you stand as ward
and pious guardian of their chastity,
as though *you* were their sire. Auspiciously
you call them queens, forgetting hostile wrath,
allowing them to keep the trappings of
their earlier lot. Your clouded countenance
and eyes made dark with tears mark out a foe
more clement than a foe, whose visage draws
aside the veil upon his soul. Such was
the force of Darius' sorrow, when he sent us,
as Alexander's clearly is as well.
Yet he mourns for his wife, you for your enemy.
Your left hand would now hold a shield, and you
would stride the battlefront; now thundering
Bucephalus would hurl you toward the foe;
now Darius would feel your fearful might
in arms, did not solicitude delay you
in burial of his wife. Let peace be made.
With no small bridal gift, the Persian king
offers you his daughter. Take all the lands
between Euphrates and the Hellespont
as bridal gift, he begs you, and accept
his daughter as the link between you both;
hold, too, his son as pledge of faith and peace.
Take as a ransom thirty thousand talents
of purest yellow gold, and let his mother
return together with the two young maidens.

"But if the gods had not endowed you with
a greater heart, and blessed your human limbs
with godlike mind, there might have been a time
you were obliged to sue for peace and fealty,
not grant it. Do you see in what great strength
Darius rushes to arms, how many races
he summons from remote lands, how the sea
is shadowed over with his fleet? The earth
is insufficient for his host's encampment,

the sea for his navy, whose waiting prows
crowd at the harbor mouths. I say no more—
the world can scarce contain this one man's strength."
[109] When Alexander had heard the messenger,
he summoned an assembly of the dukes,
taking their counsel how he should respond.
Here you might see the senate murmuring,
and long the court is said to have kept silence,
until Parmenion spoke out—although
his loyalty of spirit was not matched
by eloquence; he spoke less readily
than he performed brave deeds—"It seemed to me
that, all along, we could have profited
the most by taking ransom for those who
have either died upon the journey, or
have fled, escaping from their narrow bonds.
And now, I think, for such a weight of gold
we should exchange his aged mother and
the king's two daughters, weak civilians, who
encumber our formation and our progress.
Now by a treaty you can gain so wide
and so noble a kingdom, without loss
of life among your troops. Till now, I think,
no other man has held so many lands
that lie between Euphrates and the Danube.
But even graver matters are involved—
consider what great tasks you long to shoulder,
how huge a conquered world you leave behind.
Consider once your native land, rather
than Bactria or the Indians. After deeds
of bravery, far safer to return,
than live forever under force of arms."
[131] The Great One, bearing ill his consul's judgment,
replied, "So I too would prefer vain lucre
to victory's palm, were I Parmenion,
desiring to remain inglorious,
rather than earn the praise of victory
and yet lack wealth. But Alexander reigns
securely in the garb of poverty.
My pride lies in my kingship, not in skills

of tradesmen. Hence, all those who'd purchase Fortune!
I have no share in venal undertakings.
If captives are to be restored, I order
they be returned with gifts, no tribute asked.
No thanks ensue from benefits that follow
payment; no commerce nurtures gratitude."
[142] After he'd answered thus his consul's words,
he bade the legates enter and convey
to Darius his reply: "If I have acted
with kindness worthy of my lineage,
your king should give the credit to my nature,
not to his honor. No weak band of women
will feel my enmity. None safely scorn
Alexander, save those only whom
he scorns. I shall not wield my arms against
those who can use no arms, to whom slack weakness
of nature has denied arms. Only he
whom I consider worthy of my hatred
and wrath must arm himself. But if perchance
he'd persevered in good faith, and beseeched me
for peace by giving over all the world,
perhaps I might have felt some greater doubt
for whether I would grant it. As things stand,
he now entices my own men to treason
with bribes, and by his gift corrupts my friends
to hasten on my fate with lethal poison.
And so I shall pursue him to the death.
Against me like no honest enemy
does he plan battle, but instead he lurks,
to speak the truth, like an assassin, or
a robber armed with poisons. Now you offer
such terms of peace as seem, should I accept them,
to proffer him the palm of victory.
The dowry that you offer us consists
of all the lands across Euphrates' banks,
so that I think perhaps you have forgotten
where now we speak. Already have my ranks
crossed over the Euphrates. My camp stands
beyond the dowry's border. Drive out, then,
the Macedonian king, that he may know

those lands are yours which now you give him. Greatly
does Darius honor me, if to Mazaeus
he now prefers me as a son-in-law.
Go, carry back my answer to your tyrant:
whatever Darius has, and all he's lost,
and his own self, shall be within my power,
and fall as battle's plunder to the Greeks."
Thus he had spoken. Swiftly he dispatched
the Persians to their camp, whence Darius
enjoined Mazaeus to invade the hills
and open roads the enemy would approach.
[176] That same while, Alexander wrapped the corpse
of Darius' wife in fragrant spice, and bade
a tomb be cut into the rock's high summit,
where, famed of hand, the Jew Apelles limned
its finished surface with a wondrous scheme:
beside the names of Grecian kings, he set
the holy tales of Genesis, beginning
where first the world was born. There Matter lay,
an unformed mass, painted in varied hue,
as it brought forth four elements, each pressed
with its own seal. Here was the chain of tasks
that Godhead worked in six days: among these,
gold breathed the Daystar's splendor, ruddy gems
blazed in the heavens—thus you might have seen
the first day rise from darkness.
Here, far nobler
than creatures lacking reason, MAN IS FORMED
FROM DUST, whom his own rib deceived—that rib
seduced by lethal venom of the Serpent.
FROM EDENS VERGE THE FIERY SWORD WARDS OFF
OUR FIRST PARENTS RECEIVED BY MOTHER EARTH.
THENCE EXILED CAIN DOES NOT ESCAPE THE BOW
OF TWICE WED LAMECH. A POLLUTED RACE
SPRINGS FORTH. VIRTUE DEPARTS. VICE THRIVES. THEY CLING
TO SHAMEFUL LUSTS. TRUE PIETY GROWS SLACK.
(You might consider that Man's making grieved
the One who made him, if you were to note
the image's sad token graven here.)

NEXT AT HIS WORK THE MASTER BUILDER STANDS.
EACH LIVING RACE IS SHUT WITHIN THE ARK.
AFTER THE WAVES RECEDE THE EIGHT SURVIVORS
REPLENISH EARTH. VINEYARDS ARE PLANTED AND
THE FRUIT MAKES DRUNK THE FATHER. Rarer gold
decks out the sequence of the patriarchs:
HERE YOU MAY SEE THE AGED PARENTS LAUGH
AND ESAU HUNTING. JACOB COMES AGAIN
RETURNING WITH TWO COMPANIES. HE WRESTLES.
JOSEPHS ABDUCTION FOLLOWS NEXT. THE TRICK.
THE PRISON. AND AT LAST THE FIRST MIGRATION.
HERE EGYPT GRIEVES SMITTEN BY THE TEN PLAGUES.
THE HEBREWS PASS ACROSS. THE ROYAL KNIGHTS
PERISH. (The sea grows livid in pure gold.)
HERE MANNA FEEDS THE PEOPLE IN THE DESERT.
THE LAW IS GIVEN. FROM THE ROCK DRINK FLOWS
FOR THOSE WHO THIRST. AFTER WAR BEN-NUN
SUCCEEDS MOSES NOW BURIED. AND A NATION
IS CONQUERED. JORDANS STREAMS MOUNT IN A HEAP.
AFTER THE FLAMES OF JERICHO ACHOR
STANDS LIABLE TO THE CURSE. AND CASTING LOTS
THE SONS DIVIDE THE WORLD THEIR FATHERS LEFT THEM.
JOSHUA PAYS THE DEBT OF NATURE. LAST,
Apelles next subjects them to the Judges,
among whom SAMSON IS THE STRONGEST. YET
DELILAH BLINDS HIM ONCE HIS HAIR IS SHORN.
AND RUTH THE MOABITE HER HUSBAND LOST
BY HAPPY PLEDGE CLINGS TO THE HEBREW FOLK.

[223] A new division of the picture's space
treats of the Kings, of Eli's death, the birth
of Samuel. AT SHILOH THE PEOPLE
MURMUR. FROM BENJAMIN COMES FORTH A MAN
TO RULE THE HEBREWS. BUT BECAUSE HIS END
ILL FITS HIS ORIGINS THE SCION OF JESSE
WHO SMOTE GOLIATHS ARMS IS RAISED AS PRINCE
OVER THE PEOPLE. BUT WHEN THE TYRANT
FALLS IN THE THICK OF BATTLE WITH HIS SON
THE KINGS CURSE RAGES IN THE EMPTY HILLS.
HERE ASAHEL AND ABNER FALL. URIAH

INCURS THE DEATH HE CARRIED. IN THE TREE
THE PATRICIDE HANGS TRAPPED PIERCED BY A SPEAR.
(You might well think the father's image grieved.)
AND AFTER HE HAS SUFFERED MANS SHARED FATE
THE TEMPLE IS BUILT. WHILE THE PEACEFUL REIGNS
HIS BURIED FATHERS LAWS LIVE ON. NOR DOES
THE SACRED ALTAR SHELTER JOAB. AND
THE THIRSTY SWORD REQUIRES SHIMEIS LIFE.
UNENDING SCHISM SUNDERS LAND AND FOLK
THROUGH YOUNG MENS COUNSEL. FOR THE KINGDOMS WEALTH
CONTENTION SWELLS. Whatever either realm
does well, the skillful hand sets on the stone;
yet lest such infamy should stain the tribe,
he passes over royal idols, gods
of the one realm, Samaria's disgrace,
and Jezebel falling from the tower.
The death of Ahab and the blood-bought vines
he silently omits, nor do the fifty
perish in flames; but BY ELIJAHS SWORD
BAALS SACRED THRONG IS RAVAGED. AND IN GRIEF
THE DISCIPLE CANNOT FIND HIS MASTER.
Yet those kings whom the page proclaims as worthy
appear upon the higher register,
where HEZEKIAH SUMMONS FORTH THE LAWS
LONG DORMANT AND DESTROYS IDOLATRY.
HERE YOU MAY SEE HIS ILLNESS AND THE SUNS
RETREAT. HONORED JOSIAH CELEBRATES
THE PASSOVER. (Apart from these none reigned
in all things guiltless of apostasy,
or pure from crime.)
The prophets' images
behold! make up the higher register,
above the king and age when each one wrote.
Here to Ahaz a sign is granted, and
BEHOLD the son of Amoz here proclaims,
A VIRGIN SHALL CONCEIVE. Jeremiah
laments the city's fall under the reign
of Joachim; he says that on the earth

the Lord creates new portents, and declares
A WOMAN SHALL PROTECT A MAN. Ezechiel,
after the Gentiles take the city captive,
reveals his vision of a long-closed gate,
which signifies the virgin's untouched womb.
And Daniel prophesies CHRIST WILL BE SLAIN
AFTER SEVENTY WEEKS.
Names of twelve seers
come next, inscribed each with a prophecy
his own, and yet concordant with the rest.

[268] The last part represents great Cyrus' kingdom
and Israel's return: ZORABABEL
LEADS THEM. THE TEMPLES RESTORATION HERE
IS PAINTED. HERE THE STORY OF ESTHER
IS SHOWN FORTH AND THE CAUSE OF HAMANS DEATH
AND FOOLISH VASHTIS HAUGHTINESS. HERE SITS
TOBIAS IN THE DARKNESS ROBBED OF SIGHT.
THE MANLY JUDITH STRIKES DOWN HOLOFERNES
while with Ezra the picture's sequence ends.

[276] The customary sacrifices paid
before the tomb, now Alexander bade
the camp be swiftly struck; with rapid course
he raged against the foe, commanding Menidas,
a few men at his side, to scout the field
where now the Persians and their king lay hiding.
Mazaeus spied him from a distance, and
drew up his troops, then quickly made for camp.
But Darius, in zeal to join in battle
upon the open fields, established lines.
He wandered through the ranks, encumbering breasts
as much with admonitions as with arms.
Now the Pellaean chose a campsite, whence
the Persians' golden tents could be observed.
Now ducal ensigns flew at some small distance,
now lines stood firm. On either side you'd see
the dragons flying on the winds' light gusts.
Then Macedonian rage began to bellow,
loosing its roar into the air with raucous shouts against
the Persian host, nor did the Persians strive

to shatter heaven with less horrid clamor.
Both earth and sky shook at the sound, and Atlas
on trembling knee scarce held his endless burden.
Echo supposed the Giants waged new wars
and doubled the repeated bellowings;
the open valleys answered from hoarse throats.
The Macedonian could scarce restrain
hands laid to arms, the people in their fury;
so near the army came to breaking ranks
to rush upon the foe in frenzied madness.
[301] But now exhausted Phoebus veiled his countenance
against the sight of such a slaughter, hastening
to plunge his long-spent car into the deep.
The king gave orders to construct a palisade,
and bade the Greeks make camp in that same spot.
When in obedience they'd made embankments,
he found a knoll from which he could observe
the scattered companies of all the foe,
and see the coming peril's face entire.
There he beheld the gleaming, clanking cohorts,
the lines equipped with quivers, proud with gold;
he heard that people's garbled, barbarous murmurs;
the horses' horrid neighing struck his ears.
All this—if it is fitting to believe it—
struck fear into the man, and I imagine
fear rose with ease into that noble breast.
On such a surge of care might Typhus falter,
when Zephyr's temperate mildness guides his prow
without an oar—that breath alone suffices—
and in the placid waves the Nereid throngs
sit at their banquet; then he spies the storms
brewing off in the distance, where the South Wind
sends racing seals ahead from his deep throne,
and beats the air with dewy wings; he calls
to his companions, frees the ropes, and flies
to the rudder, leaning against the stern.
Just so, it's fitting to believe the duke,
great-hearted though he was, knew fear, beholding
those barbarous crowds whose thousands tramped the fields.

And so he summoned his own troops—perhaps
in doubt as to his course; perhaps, more likely,
to test them by his seeking of their counsel.
Parmenion's wise and long-awaited words
came forth at last: that they should seek night's help,
since they had need of stealth more than of warfare.
With ease they could drive back or kill with swords
men taken unawares by sudden chance,
checked by the blackness of the night, and sluggish
with peaceful slumber's torpor, since their languages
and customs bred confusion; or else, vanquished,
the foe would yield. But if they pressed the matter
by day, their eyes would face the hideous bodies
of Scythia's race, and ugly, unshorn Indians,
the Bactrians' and Giants' towering height;
those loathly forms could crush hearts with vain fear.
He further pointed out that so few men
could not surround nor drive so many thousands
from field of battle; Darius, furthermore,
had occupied wide, level plains, and chosen
not to decide the battle once again
amidst Cilicia's narrow mountain passes.

[347] Nearly as one, the Macedonian ranks
praised and approved the plan, and Polipercon
declared that in the advantage of the night
lay triumph for the Greeks. The king looked toward him
—for still he did not venture to accuse
Parmenion, or haughtily affront him;
so he assailed him now with bitter satire,
though just before he'd asked him for his counsel:
"In this you recommend a robber's habits,
the cleverness of thieves, whose single hope
and chief desire is to do harm through treachery,
and to deceive by hidden fraud. Our glory
shall wage no war of trickery. Narrow defiles,
Cilicia's passes, slothful Darius' absence,
the furtive suffrance of the timid night—
all these I scorn, lest any blackened stain
obscure the brightness of my fame. By day

I shall go forward to meet men. The victory
we win by swords must come with honor, or
not come at all. Better a king should grieve
his failing lot, than be shamed by a triumph
brought forth from night. Conquest is not so precious
that I would wish posterity to read
I'd conquered by a plot, or that mere scheming
should slight the victor's palm. Indeed, we know
the Persians stand watch, lest their well-armed ranks
should be deceived with falsehood by the foe.
Therefore, restore your bodies' strength with sleep
in preparation for the work of day,
and keep in mind the approaching dawn's commotions,
which will subject to you half of the world."
The warrior spoke, and turned back to the tents.

[374] Behind opposing lines, with no less zeal
Darius prepared the Persian troops and armed them,
imagining that the enemy would act
as though Parmenion's counsel had prevailed.
The horses gnashed their bits, the food of rage,
and gleaming trappings shone upon their backs.
The lines blazed out like strings of kindled fires,
and helmets vied with stars; the lofty ether,
reflected from the shields, met equal flames,
and feared lest earth were laboring to be heaven.
The night rejoiced to bear the guise of day,
while Darius' helmet thought to play the sun,
in strife with Phoebus: on its highest crest
was set a fiery lamp that blocked night's stars
and yielded to the sun alone, indignant,
outshining others by the same degree.
A thousand stones flashed 'round it, and each one
gave forth the blazing light of carbuncles.

[391] Struck by the swift commotion, either host
was overcome by monstrous fear. Upon
a gilded bed, the second Jove reclined
but could not sleep, his royal form enveloped
in anxious care. Now from the mountain's height
he sent the Greeks against the right flank. Now

he broke the lines upon the left, and now
assayed head-on attack against the foe,
eluding scythes fixed on the wheels of chariots.
He passed a sleepless night in contemplation
of myriad cares his breast could not contain.
[401] Amidst the Tiber's swift, divided stream,
there lies an island worthy of all reverence.
By virtue of its site, it claims the head
both of world and empire; and upon
its foursquare columns, rising in the air
beneath the incline of the moon's high course,
there stands the palace of the queen called Victory.
A thousand doors give access; at the touch
it clatters with a thousand tinkling gemstones,
and once a hinge is bent, the whole world hears
its whispering. Upon the foremost threshold,
wakeful AMBITION, mother of all cares,
mutters and guards the entrance, while within,
the goddess sits upon an ivory throne,
and laurel presses her triumphant locks.
Her hand is ever generous. At her sides,
her sisters and companions always flank her,
and give adornment to those royal halls:
GLORY, forever living, sings immortal
songs in lyric strain, while MAJESTY
disdains the ages with her proud contempt,
and REVERENCE becalms the docile peoples.
JUSTICE, who arms the laws and safeguards right,
is there as well, unswayed by gifts, and CLEMENCY
sits near at hand to keep the kingdom stable,
she who alone has pity on the wretched,
and teaches mercy for the vanquished. LUCRE
stands by, the source of vice, mother of excess,
uncouth despite her wealth, while near her, CONCORD
lays rest to hatred, offering her kisses
with placid countenance to all the rest.
There too is PEACE, and PLENTY with full horn.
Those who delight the goddess with their pleasures,
mingling their jest with weighty matters, sit

before them all, Applause, and flattering Laughter,
who stammers his deceits, and wavering Favor:
their mirth offers the goddess salutations,
and instruments sound forth the Muse's numbers.
[433] The goddess, then, beheld the Great One turning
so many cares within his breast, to whom
from infancy she'd granted constant triumphs.
She feared the coming battle's wrack perchance
would overwhelm his sleepless limbs. At once
she sprang up, veiled in cloud, approached the caves
where all lay quiet, and Sleep held his court.
"Father, arise," she said, "descend upon
the Macedonian king where now he lies,
and loose his soul and body from their cares."
She'd spoken. Heavily, and scarcely shaking
his recent slumber from his frame, he lifted
his madid feathers to the upper air.
Along his course, stars touched by Lethe's liquor
forgot their usual wanderings and slept.
And so with sluggish flight he reached the Greeks.
He lay full-length upon the prince's couch
to drive away the swarm of cares, and soaked
his bones with dew of poppies to the marrow.
A deeper sleep then pressed on the king's spirit,
and held him whom anxiety had vexed,
until beneath the Hyperborean Wain
night's darkness shrank away, stars languished, and
swift Lucifer set lamps amidst the ether.
[454] Bearing the presage of that woe-filled day,
the Titan rose from Nabataean waves
with lurid countenance. In dawn's new light
the Grecian princes gathered near the king,
and marveled that, against his wont, he lolled
inside his chamber, when at other times
he'd roused the very watchmen, goading on
the sluggish, hastening those who tarried; yet
when greatest danger loomed, pressing both hosts
with fate's wild blast, the youth, to their amazement,
lay freed from care and motionless in slumber.

Among them there were those who risked believing
he cloaked his fear in shadow, lying hidden
though sleep had not come over him. His guards
were fearful to intrude or to approach him,
nor would they arm themselves, unless his voice
commanded them to march; without the prince
no soldier dared advance. Parmenion
devised a useful plan, lest any circumstance
delay the battle. He ordered that the tribunes
should arm themselves and take some nourishment.
Already movements of the other host
left no choice but to advance, and so at last
the duke approached the king's bed, still unable
to rouse him with his oft-repeated words.
A gentle hand awoke him. "The dawn's up,"
he said. "Shake off these languid dreams. How can
such torpor seize you, when the Medes approach
so closely in their columns? Now the foe
sends out advancing troops, Bellona rages,
and yet your unarmed ranks await your orders.
Your soul's courage, the rigor of your strength,
which never broke or sank, where are they now?
Before, you were accustomed to arouse
the watchmen's hearts when they were dull with sleep."
Mars' hero then replied, "Be well assured
that never did I dream, before my breast
reposed unburdened of its heavy cares."
Vast wonder seized the duke, that Alexander
had claimed his heart stood free of care; and yet
he dared not seek the reason. But the king
continued: "Then I have just cause for fear,
when Darius flees and fires his towns behind him,
consuming villages and wasting fields:
then were my restless mind weighed down with cares.
But now, when Darius and all his host
present themselves in arms before me, nor
can they seek flight in order to escape,
my fear subsides. Why, then, do I delay?

Go, make the customary preparations.
Another time I'll say all this at leisure."

[498] He spoke, at trumpet's call bidding the Greeks
to arm themselves, and fixed his own equipment
upon his limbs. Scale-armor worked in bronze
descended, winding downward, to his feet.
And next there came the spur, made to plant wings
on sluggish hooves, and with its biting tooth
to castigate delay: thus, if his voice
or horn's blast could not rouse his ambling mount,
as he attempted to head off the course
of those who fled, at least the beast might heed
the harsh goads laid upon his flank. A mail-coat
with triple-woven links hung from his head
to guard that noble breast and his smooth shoulders;
it circled shapely elbows with hooked arm holes,
but spared his eyes, that he might see his foe.
A brazen helmet sat upon his head,
blazing with fiery crests, to safeguard doubly
the human frame's most worthy part. A sword,
soon to shed streams of blood by its dire carnage,
hung at his side, and by its agency
the chambers of black Hades hoped to fill
their empty shrines with ghosts. Now Bucephal
was led out. When the king had leapt astride him,
the world's fierce conqueror conquered all his fierceness;
his left hand wed the shield by happy compact,
while yet with equal love it held the reins.
Upon his ashen spear a bright point gleamed;
its flaming pennant's lion lashed the stars.
From Mars' first contest, never had his men
beheld him show more zeal. Now strode the Great One
into their midst, and vigorous hope revived
the flagging ranks, as victory filled his face.

[526] And so he set divisions to the columns,
arranging battle lines in their due order.
He bade them break formation and flow outward,
in order to avoid the scythe-wheeled chariots,

in which lay Darius' only hope of triumph;
but they should overwhelm the charioteers
and horses, lest they fly past unimpeded.
While still he briefed his men and fortified them,
there broke through a deserter from the Persians,
who brought news to the king that Darius
had laid upon the earth with hidden cunning
iron devices shaped like murex shells:
if strength alone could not subdue his foe,
he hoped to hold them back with clinging hooks,
and plunge the Grecian troops in hidden ruin.
[539] The king commanded him to show his men
the place where Babylon's lord had imitated
Ulysses' cleverness and laid the hooks,
but bade him be detained, against the chance
the Persian's lying speech should snare his men.
He ordered that the spot be pointed out
to all, and that its fraud was to be shunned,
lest treachery should undermine high virtue.
But then, going before their teeming ranks,
he roused his men to combat by his words
and eloquent gestures: "O comrades, now
before your hands, behold your final task.
The battle on the stream of Granicus,
the victory in Cilicia's narrow passes—
what praise or honor have they still, unless
our god and Fortune cap our one last triumph
with favorable outcome? But Fortune *is* that god
who, ever fostering Alexander's strength,
delights to hold her sceptre under me,
just as all other great men reign beneath
her mighty sway. From that time when Greece first
beheld me at the reins of Macedonia,
she gave my men her favor, and though many
desire our harm, yet none will dare attempt it.
This vast host holds no danger but its numbers,
for to this end has Fortune labored, that
once and for all the world is mine to conquer:
Fortune has tired of counting lesser triumphs.

Our victory will be the worthier,
in that we wrest it from far greater numbers.
Press through their weakling ranks, your blades before you.
You see how shields obscure a sun reflected
by gems and gold, how purple cloaks the fields.
Who would not wish for such a battle's victory?
Who but an idiot would spurn that gold?
The gathered riches of the Orient,
the Arabs' toil, is ripe here for the plucking.
If blades obey the mind, if sword blows match
the greed of hearts, if spirits lust for slaughter,
and thirst for gore just as they thirst for gold,
then all you see is yours, nor will I claim it.
Only conquer for me, and then among you
divide the spoils. He who prevails with me
will share with me the praise; but take the rest.
Take Alexander as your power's exemplar,
your model in Mars' combat: if the king
fails to appear foremost among the vanguard,
or turns his back upon the foe, those fleeing
will merit pardon; they'll have full excuse
who go forth sluggishly. But if nowhere
do I fail to advance, and never say
to brave men, "Go, go first," but rather can be seen
preceding all the rest in arms, then finally
am I worthy to have my comrades follow.
Let him who rules move brave men by example,
and show the teachings of his own prowess."
He'd spoken, and the battle lines converged.
Such din and shouting of the masses rose
into the ether, as though ancient Chaos
had roused its former strife to claim again
the world's failing machine; had caused the elements,
struck when the fetters of all things were broken,
to lift their horrid clangor to the stars.

Book Five

The Headings of the Fifth Book

The fifth book treats of ruin, and of deaths
bewept by close survivors. Darius
at Arbela considers adverse Fortune;
he counsels vanquished Persians to trust Fate
once more, when strength's regained, in Media's realms.
The princes hesitate. Aeacus' scion
summons the ranks, and heals their wounds with gifts.
Illustrious Mazaeus and his offspring,
after the ranks have passed, escort the king
inside the lofty walls of Babylon.

Book Five

According to the law King Numa set
in days of old to fix the months in order,
the fifth descended now from two-faced Janus
to mark the flowering year with rosy hue,
and Leda's sons with doubled shouts of joy
received Phoebus as guest. A new day dawned
upon the clash of princes, soon to bring
destruction to the Persians and the Medes—
so Daniel is believed to have foreseen
and written down obscurely; heaven's vengeance
was now at hand, and from dry northern regions
the goat had come—the mighty son of Philip.
    [11] From far off, Aristomenes of India

caught sight of him, his fiery helmet gleaming,
and lashed his elephant with ten-fold blows.
He spared no force, but plunged his venomed sword point
into the shield; the mail-coat turned its force
and saved the flesh within. The Great One launched
an arrow at the monster, and the point
cut through its vital entrails, where the trunk
and flank were joined. The monster in its fall
roared hideously, and, when it had collapsed,
the avenging sword, incapable of mercy,
left Aristomenes without his head.
"Ours, ours the victory!" the Greeks kept shouting.
The Persians drew together, and thick showers
of missiles rained about the king; but neither
javelin nor axe dislodged the hero,
whom guiding Fortune shielded with strong virtue.
[26] Unconquerable and tireless, he burst
through mingled swords and spears, giving no quarter,
and like an iron hammer struck against
limbs sheathed in armor. While he thus raged on,
his spear felled Eliphaz, the son of Pharaon,
a Syrian who fought on foot, while Pharos,
Orcanus' son, a knight from Egypt, died
upon his sword point. Ground long dry and sterile
grew moist now with a river of spilt blood,
and waves of gore pulsed through the veins of Cybele.
A countless band of Persians and of Greeks
fell in their turns. Enos and Caynan lay
slain by Philotas' sword—Enos, whose sword
had struck Hesiphilus, Caynan, whose axe
brought death to Laomedon.
[38] Now Geon rallied
to deal a lethal wound to Alexander,
had Fortune willed it. Horrible of face,
a dweller on the Red Sea, he was thought
to be the offspring of a Giant mother,
who'd born him to her Ethiopian husband.
In towering bulk he took after his mother,
but had the swart complexion of his sire;

those whom his blackness could not terrify
were awestruck by his frame. His knotted club
destroyed some fifteen men, as on a path
towards the Great One through the Grecian columns
he burst along a twisting whirlwind path,
like the Nemean Boar, whose razor teeth
tear at the hounds: its lips are smeared with froth,
and on its back the bristles form a palisade,
as over all the dogs its shoulders tower.
He thundered now against some on the left,
now on the right against still others; some
he butted with his head around the kidneys,
then twisted to the other side, defending
his either flank with swiftly whirling movements.
He came thus to the king. Mars' hero saw him,
and wondered at his size. The Giant raised
his gory club, and thundered at the king
from rumbling throat: "What frenzy drives you, Great One,
against a Giant foe? You've read we strove
to gain the starry citadels of Jupiter,
and scarcely did his lightning bolt preserve
the son of Saturn on his heavenly throne."
He'd not yet finished, when a pine-shaft, thrown
by Alexander's vigorous arm, stood fixed
inside the speaker's mouth, nailing his tongue
against his jaws, and checking further blasphemy.
Yet still he stood and chewed the bloody weapon,
till Alexander saw the open quarter,
and dashed his horse's breast against him, casting
his limbs upon the earth that bore his race.
So mothering earth bewailed her fallen progeny,
and echoed with such din, as when an oak
is twisted from its proud and ancient roots
by Boreas' violent breath upon the mountains.
The Argive ranks ran up and thrust their lances
through Geon's flesh; his entrails felt their swords.
They sent him to the caves of Acheron,
his face in shreds, his breast a field of wounds.
    [76] Elsewhere, illustrious Clitus raged against

the Parthian columns. (But I judge it better
to pass over in silence what reward
he gained for all his merits, though his sister
had nursed the Great One at her breast.) When Sanga,
a warrior of Damascus, saw him splattered
with blood his brother had shed, three times he groaned,
moved by fraternal love, and doubled sighs
from deep within his breast choked off his voice.
He cast three javelins to sate his frenzy,
and still his heart was burdened. With drawn sword
he leapt down from his gleaming car, and struck
the head of Clitus, where his flashing helmet
blazed with its carbuncle. Had not his neck
been safely shielded by the mail-coat's cap,
it would have mourned his savaged brain, since now
the helm lay shattered. Loss of blood amazed him,
and yet he smartly anwered Sanga's blade:
the iron that had pierced one brother's entrails
now bathed deep in the midriff of the second.
Their father Mecha saw them being slaughtered.
At first he grew stiff, and no rain of tears
flowed on his face, for grief within absorbed them,
and showers suited to his aged countenance
instead dropped on his heart's dry chambers. Thus
his weeping breast fulfilled his eye's due offices.
At last, his blood revived, his mind returned,
and though sobs interrupted his laments,
"Most savage of tormentors," he began,
"has your sword now devoured both of these brothers,
each in his father's sight, with no regard
for how you've sped their aged sire's days,
and those of their poor mother? Raging tiger,
no further crime should check you. That same iron
with which you broke my heart, as I looked on,
should join the father to his sons. Send back
three biers of lamentation, sons and husband,
to one who grieves as mother and as spouse.
But if you have a wife, a son and heir,
or sister, or a mother, may they grieve

for that same vengeful thread spun by the Fates
for which I grieve. May they mourn as I sorrow."
He spoke, and with his weakened right hand cast
his spear at Clitus' face. It scarcely stuck
upon the boss, as Clitus shook it off;
then where the thick and venerable white hair
ran toward the shoulders, with his lethal blade
he pierced that hoary throat. Mecha fell down,
a wretched sight, between his half-dead sons.
Embracing both his offspring, then he passed
towards the infernal city with his sons.
[123] Marked out by regal excess, Darius' column
itself approached, and from his lofty chariot
the king gleamed forth. A blaze of countless gems
revealed the king's own person, and Nicanor
was struck dumb by the light. He was commander
upon the left flank; now he sent the wedge
that marched beneath his sway towards that brilliance.
Upon his first endeavors Fortune smiled;
seductively she led Parmenion's scion
amidst his rage. The wave of the first onslaught
could scarce oppose him, only barely holding
against Nicanor's steady line, until
the Arab Remnon violently rushed in,
surrounded by a storm of fighters. He
stayed those who fled, and roused their flagging minds.
They took a stand and planted steady feet.
Far off men fell by sling and javelin,
close up by sword and brain-smeared axe, while infantry
dispatched their task with gory stakes and spits
wielded in hate. The greedy seats of Hades
and all the shadowy cavern's empty houses
were overflowing, nor could just one sister
break all those threads, but Clotho and Lachesis
threw down their tasks: two sisters helped the third
mow down the fates of countless dying men.
[145] Both peers and commons perished on each side,
but yet Nicanor shone with special praise
among the princes for his many slaughters.

Through ranks of Persians who surrounded Remnon
he tracked him, counting his own deeds for nought,
though he had wasted thousands, while he spied
the lord and master of those troops still living.
The throngs fell back, as on the two men came.
A hideous roar assailed the stars, and screams
of men beset the fields. Their iron-shod horses
tore up the crumbling turf. Now they gained quarter,
and came to closer combat. Each discerned
the favor of the gods in his first strike,
and neither was unhorsed, though savagely
each felt the blow the maple lance had dealt.
The hand left idle now sought out the sword hilt.
From under shattered helmets, blood poured out
in streams upon the field, and shields gave way
before the angry blades. Their knees gone slack,
mounts fell, and riders too. Parmenion's son
was first to draw his sword and rise again.
He pressed down Remnon's chest with both his knees,
until he'd plunged his weapon to the hilt
into the Parthian's inmost vital organs.
    [166] At once the shaken Arabs left the contest,
and turned their backs for flight; but then arrived
a countless band of warriors, whom Hyrcania
had bred for excellence in Mars' fierce strife.
They took a stand and walled Nicanor off,
surrounding him with a hedge of crashing arms.
Their spears first overwhelmed him. Rocks and sling-stones
rang on his helmet, and his broken shield
was dumbstruck to behold a grove of oak
established in its cracks. His feet and forearms
now failed him, and his limbs were drenched in blood
mingled with sweat. Yet his unbroken virtue,
the princely courage of his mind, still governed
his captive breast. Assailed by spears and slings,
that wall of Alexander fell at last,
but not without abiding reputation:
his ruinous overthrow brought on the fall
of many Persians, just as in the city

of Romulus, a tower, when it crashes,
brings down a nearby house with thunderous whirling.
[183] Meanwhile, the bitter wailing of the Greeks
assailed the Macedonian, who flew forward
more fiercely than a bear who's lost her cubs.
The crowd who faced that Deluge of the World
quaked at the prince's onslaught, and then fled
headlong through trackless wastes, fully determined
to choose life over triumph. Only Fidias,
the son of Mennon, faced down Alexander
while others fled. His face vied with fresh snow,
and on his rosy cheeks the first down sprouted.
He drew his noble blood from Cyrus' line,
and Darius' sister was his promised bride.
Here were grounds for pride, if Mars' bright glory
would fall to him; he made towards the Great One.
But neither wealth, nor youth's advantage, nor
the lustre of his ancestry could stay death.
Hephaestion, his equal by his beauty
but marked for disparate fate, rode toward the youth
with loosened rein, and where a brazen tiger
breathed flame upon the boss, he clove the shield.
The iron mail-coat gaped, its links undone,
to grant an entry to the brilliant blade.
A shaft ran through his breast's dark hiding places.
His snowy neck bent back against his shoulders;
the shadow of perpetual night spread over him,
his eyes now closed in an eternal sleep.
[205] But on the left flank, where Parmenion
held the command, second to none in warfare,
fractious Bellona raged, her locks all drenched
with recent gore, her tresses smeared with clots.
Her brother sped amidst dire storms to meet her,
his chariot flecked with blood, his eyes aflame,
like lightning and the crash of thunder. FURY
prepared his paths, and cowardly spirits fled
before her onslaught. WRATH, her near companion,
rushed headlong, scorning REASON's humble reins
with gall-filled eye; IMPULSE, who flouts delay

and orders all things badly, overturned
the cars athwart their path. Success and failure
flew everywhere commingled; from Mars' head
a thousand deaths trembled in empty air
with pallid countenance. The horrid god
thus laid his arms about his sister's neck
as they embraced. "Swiftly descend, dear sister,"
he said. "Thus charge the Macedonian king:
'You're led by futile hope, if in your ignorance
you mean yourself to finish Darius.
The gods have kept this crime from such a prince,
nor is it lawful for the hand that wields
the sceptre of the world to drip polluted
with slaughter of old men. Another Fortune
is owed to Darius, who'll fall by treason
among his own. Go, then, to meet Mazaeus,
swift and implacable through hostile arms:
he wastes the Greeks with varied slaughter, lusting
for Macedonian plunder, and releasing
the Persians from their shackles, while in turn
he lays chains on the Greeks. Parmenion
can hold no longer with his scanty ranks
against so many thousands.'" Thus he spoke,
and, faster than the South Wind full of showers,
she passed with crashing toward the right-hand flank,
assuming Pallas' face and hideous arms,
upon her shield the Gorgon's snake-haired visage.
She briefly set the god's commands before him,
then vanished in a cloud of noxious poison.
    [241] The Macedonian followed in a leap,
and hurled these words after the fleeing goddess:
"No matter from what quarter of the world
you've come, goddess, we spurn your futile omen.
Though Atlas' tireless and wind-footed scion
should be sent from on high, to bring report
the Persians held my mother and my sisters,
he'd not deflect me from the car of Darius.
On him depends our only hope of victory;
him if I shall destroy, I count for little

whatever may be lost; him if alone
I conquer, he alone restores my losses.
The loss of what can be regained is negligible,
next to the hope that I might conquer him.
Neither shall Fortune snatch him from me, though
a tower shield Darius with sevenfold wall,
though Acheron defend the ramparts, flowing
with blazing waves between its sulfurous banks."
He took a stand in arms when he had spoken.
His shoulder pressed the shield, as to the wall
of his great breast he set that blazoned rampart.
He raised his shaft of pine towards the stars;
its tip aloft, he rushed amidst the foe
with foe's intent, and swirling clouds of dust
bore witness Alexander was at hand.
Affer, the son of Ariston, was slain—
his lance lay in the dust—and Lysias
was trampled by the hooves of horses. Affer
had come from Libya's reefs, the tetrarch Lysias
from frosty Scythia; Craterus slew
the first, Amyntas cast down Lysias,
who fell by sword, while spear point claimed the other.
Amulon joined them both, his gaping throat
exhaling reddened breath. Antigonus
laid Baradas upon the heap, and Ptolemy
pressed back the throngs of knights. Nor was the glory
of Coenus or Eumenidus' dire strife
less than your own, Meleager. Perdicas
pressed at the very line of Darius
more fiercely than his wont, while all beheld him.
Polipercon, who'd previously contended
that victory lay in night, redeemed by day,
in sight of all, that earlier nighttime counsel.
The youth of Argos raged with one resolve:
all felt a single fury, and like courage
marked each as mirror image of his lord.
Thus Alexander, if he chanced to glimpse
his fellows' martial rage from near at hand,
might thrill to see himself so often doubled.

The victor's roar now struck the ears of Darius,
and storms of death burst on his closest comrades.
[283] Adversity left faint the wise man's spirit;
faint counsel could he offer to himself,
while hope languished defenseless, and remorse
for earlier undertakings now consumed him.
Which way should Darius turn? Amidst his madness
how should he rule himself, when flight's not safe,
nor may he find companions, if he tarries?
Of many thousands whom he'd earlier trusted,
scarcely a thousand had survived the war
to shield their country. Shame and reputation
forbade his flight, yet trepidation urged it.
But while his wavering breast still trembled, dumbstruck,
while yet he half resolved to take his flight,
or else, in hatred of his life, to welcome
his captor's chains, the Persians turned their backs
almost as one, as though still in formation,
and rushed across the fields, leaving their king.
Unwillingly, at last he loosed the reins
upon the horse he'd seized, and so retreated
through lands bedewed with slaughter of his men.
Doomed king, where will your aimless flight direct you?
You know not, lost man, whom you flee, you know not,
but run to meet your foe while foe you flee.
You fall to Scylla while you shun Charybdis.
Bessus, Narbazanes, your wealth's great sharers,
feel no dread breaking fealty, though you raised
them both to princely rank from lowly station;
but spurning all the governance of law,
in their lord's death—great shame!—these slaves conspire.
They'll slay your reverend head for all its whiteness.
[307] When Alexander heard that from death's threshold
Darius had escaped, he flew, still bloodied,
across the bones of kings, tracking the fugitive
in great leaps over piled corpses, scorning
in his abandon nearly all companions.
Just so, a rushing star will trail its flames,
marking the clouds with intermittent fire;

just so, the Rhône bursts forth from Alpine rocks
high at its spewing source, there where Maximian
slew Eastern troops: the wave of blood augmented
the river's stream, and mingled gore burst upwards
towards the heights, scorning earthen banks;
the Theban legion's death drenched all Agaunum.
[319] But, headlong through the trackless, rocky wastes,
the son of Belus now crossed Lycus' stream
with few companions, hesitating whether
to smash the bridge that lay across the torrent,
and so to close the route to the Pellaean.
He feared his men would face the foe's fierce carnage,
if he should cut the Persian columns off
to gain safe flight by pulling down the bridge.
Respect for honor overcame utility,
as Darius set his men above himself.
A just man, he preferred to turn his back
upon a road left open to the victor,
rather than close it off before the vanquished.
The Persians fled, dashing in scattered ranks
from everywhere towards the bridge. But thirst,
redoubled by intolerable heat,
and by their course's speed, seared weakened entrails.
Sweat drenched exhausted limbs, and hoarse gasps wracked
their trembling lungs. Thus, desperate for water,
they sought the flowing rills of hidden moisture
deep in the trackless groves. On every bank
they lay, and greedily drank the muddy torrents,
until their organs stiffened with the muck.
Their bellies swelled like wombs of pregnant women,
and bore in travail death the streams had sired.
The fluid blocked the vital passages
of those who'd guzzled with a greedy throat,
trapping the air deep in the breast's blind caverns.
Meanwhile, the narrow span of that lone bridge
could not accommodate so many throngs
of princes or of common rank and file,
who rushed toward death, with fear their only guide.
The whirling channel with its swollen waves

could scarce receive the crowds. They fell in droves,
until the river's void enveloped them:
the green Nymphs wondered at the mounting corpses.
[350] Now Phoebus' horses ran the final slope
of high Olympus. Ethiopia's fields
lay smoking, while the sun's proximity
burned Herculean Gades now more gently.
The Macedonian saw his men's blunt weapons
and their exhausted swords. Since then the hour
rushed headlong into night, he bent his course
to where he knew his men stood on the left front.
But as he turned his arms in that direction,
a knight sent by Parmenion announced
his triumph, and the vexed foe's mingled rout.
He led the knights back into the encampment,
but suddenly a Persian column burst
forth from a valley, searing all the fields
with fire from gleaming shields and helmets. Stopping
at first with halted step, at length they saw
how few the Macedonians were in number,
and turned their gory lines against the Great One.
The king advanced before his soldiers' banners,
as was his wont, not so much scorning danger
in warfare as ignoring it. He set
against the Medes the encampment of his breast,
so many times besieged, yet still insuperable,
nor did his constant Fortune then desert him
in wavering circumstance. He seized their leader,
who raged amidst his troops in love of death
and warfare, till the swift sword clove his guts.
Immediately Lysimachus and the glory
of all the Grecian race assailed the Arabs
on every side, and Mars spared neither army
his fury: there no man lay unavenged.
[376] But when the star of Atlas' scion dared
to match the rays of Phoebus with his countenance,
the Persians trusted flight over Mars' contest,
and broke their ranks, escape their only thought.
With freely loosened reins, they crossed near midnight

the river's flow, thence reaching Arbela's walls.
There Babylon's sad and distracted king
took counsel for the harshness of their fortunes
with those whom he had carried into flight.
When he had checked his heart's sighing laments,
he gazed with tearful eye on those scant remnants
of Argive wrath. "The human lot," he said,
"turns endlessly amidst tumultuous chance,
to suffer in adversity, and then
to rally under favorable circumstance,
to bend the head to ills and then to raise it.
So Lydia beheld a humbled Croesus;
so in her turn a lady pressed the victor.
Thermopylae beheld a prostrate Xerxes,
and he whose navy covered all the sea
could scarce return with one ship from defeat.
No novelty should overwhelm brave hearts,
since not for long is Fortune ever held
by any law of fealty to a man.
The sole hope of the conquered lies in wresting
the victory once again from conquering hands.
No doubt the victor will advance on fields
and cities emptied of their folk, but crammed
with gold and other riches. There, a nation
unmatched in greed will guzzle with wide throat
that lethal metal: they will try to slake
the thirst of their dry entrails with fresh plunder,
and so to sate the hunger they've conceived.
We stand to gain by such events, I think.
Meanwhile, I'll seek the borderlands that war
has never touched, the farthest realms of Media,
there to restore my strength to fullness. Great men
have learned by long experience what burdens
are placed on warriors by rich household goods,
by camps that swell with eunuchs and with courtesans.
The Macedonian will be the weaker,
when such things are shared out, than previously,
when still he lacked them all. Laden with spoils,
he'll be subdued, though destitute he conquered.

War's waged with steel, not gold. Not towns nor coin
protect a kingdom, but courage and strength.
So let us seek the distant Median territories.
Our very capability of doing so,
though unappealing, teaches us, amidst
adversity, to follow useful counsel.
Our ancient fathers in their first endeavors
were thus afflicted by the ills of chance;
and yet we know that, when a few days passed,
they healed their Fortune and beat back the foe,
and from their adverse lot again seized triumph."

[422] So Darius concluded. But his words
seemed full of fear and trembling to his men:
soon Alexander would break rich Babylon
and all the cities of the farthest East,
which now stood undefended. Further chance
to make amends for Fortune scarce seemed likely,
nor any means to hold onto the kingdom.
Yet, strengthened in resolve—or else obedient,
heeding their duke's command more than his counsel—
they hastened with one mind toward Media.

[431] Without delay, the Macedonian
from open hand doled Arbela's vast treasure,
until the army felt the burden, and
their greed was sated by the recent plunder.
Traversing Syria swifter than storms
borne on the South Wind, vanquishing its citizens
by force or friendship, now he burned to pierce
the baked-brick walls, and gain the palaces
inside that city marked by praise of kings,
which drew its lasting fame from tongue's confusion.
From Semiramis' town he stood as far
as Saint-Denis lies from the Seine's broad waters,
when lo! that noble man Mazaeus, and
his much-loved son, came forward as deserters,
surrendering themselves and Babylon
to Alexander's sway. The king embraced him
in eagerness and great benevolence:
his silent vows were heaped upon his joy,

for not without long toil and preparation
could such a town be taken in a siege,
strong as its towers and its numbers made it,
unless devices of a godlike strength
would crack its mortared joints with constant blows.
That man of ready hand, distinguished by
his earlier battles' glory, tried of arms
so many times, served others as example
to enter into compacts of sure peace.
The ranks were drawn up tightly, and the Persians
were ordered to give quarter and to follow;
the astonished town received the foursquare columns.

[456] At such a king's advent, all Babylon shone,
setting in view the wealth heaped by the shrewdness
of ancient kings. The altars blazed with gems,
and veils were taken from ancestral effigies
in sacred porticoes, while silken banners
laughed in the breeze on squares, in streets and crossroads.
The temples blazed with garlands that flashed gold,
while matrons grave of mien and sober citizens
glowed in silk garments picked with broidered monsters.
Handmaids and slaves, when ordered to shine forth
with barbarous luxury, could not sustain
such unaccustomed garb: as they beheld
those vestments, they forgot their rightful station,
supposing they'd no longer be called slaves.
Those whom deceitful wealth had overlooked
shone in their borrowed clothes among the honored.
The loveliness of blooms and verdant branches
stripped from the trees bestrewed the victor's path,
and everywhere frankincense vied with odor
from fragrant woods of Araby, which fed
the holy fires, and filled the nostrils with
their morningtide aroma. Savage tigers
were carried forth, outraged at their imprisonment,
along with leopards dragged from iron cages,
while horrid lions roared inside their dens,
and all the beasts that haunt Hyrcanian groves.
Lest close-packed crowds impede their gaze, men climbed

with steady gait atop the roofs in eagerness
to own their king, and countless standing throngs
crowned lofty walls in lines. The jesters ran
forward to sing their songs in lyric strains,
accompanied by harps, while cymbals rang
along with sistrum, psaltery, and drum,
and bowed vielles were there to lull men's ears.
The seers of Memphis adored the victor's car—
those whom the lies of the Egyptian race
claim know the stars and Fate's unswerving course,
and tell what is to come by heaven's portent.
[491] Never did boastful Rome receive her victor
with adulation of so fine a triumph,
not when at Leucas Caesar struck down Antony,
and Cleopatra's breasts gave suck to asps—
thereby he changed the sixth month's name—nor when
the blood of mighty Pompey sated Julius,
who went forth from Emathia's battlefield
to break Tarpeius' citadel. And rightly:
for if you recollect the wondrous deeds
of kings, and praise them justly by their titles;
if you recall with what a meager host
the Macedonian approached such deeds,
in flower of tender youth, against world conquerors,
and in how brief a time the whole world lay
before the knees of Alexander—then
that whole array of dukes will seem mere rabble,
whether the men the Spanish poet sings
with high-flown melody, or those whom Claudian
distinguishes by his lofty verses' strains.
Lucan would blush to sing his victory-song
for Caesar and the fall of Rome; Honorius
would yield to Macedonia's bright arms.
If pious prayers and tearful lamentation
moved mercy from on high to grant the Franks
a king like this, the True Faith would shine forth
unhindered through the earth, and Parthia,
broken by our arms, would beg unbidden
for baptism's renewal, while high Carthage,

which long lay ruined, soon would rise again
at mention of Christ's name. The penalties
that Spain deserved to pay under great Charles
would be exacted by the cross's banners,
and every race and tongue would sing of Jesus,
and freely would approach the holy font
under Reims' holy bishop's tutelage.

Book Six

The Headings of the Sixth Book

The sixth book shows an Alexander corrupted
by Babel's gilded luxury. He sets
fixed military payments. With armed host
he meets the Uxii. He frees the city
at Sisigambis' prayer. Persepolis smokes
from fallen walls. A band of wretches moves
the king. Darius prepares again for war.
Sedition parts the parricides from Darius;
inbred suspicions reconcile them to him,
nor can Patron's advice change Fate's decree.

Book Six

Behold the world's one scourge, its kings' sole terror;
behold, O Babylon, the goat foretold
upon the Sacred Page, where many times
you might have read of Asia's conqueror,
who'd break the double kingdom's horns. Now marvel
at his presence: mock not that he's shut
within your walls of brick, for he embraces
the whole broad world, and at his name's mere sound
kings tremble. He will be your sovereign,
whom all the earth might choose as sovereign,
had he endured in that same virtuous mien
with which his power began. See with what kindness

his rein lies on the vanquished; see the clemency
the victor shows amidst so much success;
see how mildly he dispenses justice
to the nations, owning those as citizens
who were his foes in war, and conquering
with love those whom he'd conquered first in battle.
[16] The schooling that impressed once-tender youth
had taught the true adornment of the soul,
the lineaments of life's perfection. Yet
the wealth of Babylon, the slothful pleasures
its populace enjoyed, made slack the workings
of inborn virtue's rigor. Vile corruption
stained all that city's customs; unmixed wine
warmed every heart to Venus' venal evils.
Men pimped their wives, and parents their own children,
provided only sin was paid its price.
By night the banquets saw those solemn revels
that tyrants keep by long ancestral wont.
Four days and thirty, Alexander lingered
amidst the idle wantonness of Babylon;
his troops, who would subdue the world, were weaker
for such a stay, had an unbridled foe
burst in upon the slothful banqueters.
[33] Mars' hero quit Semiramis' broad lands,
and set up camp in Satrapene's fields.
He judged that former ordinances of warfare,
established by his fathers, should be changed.
He wisely set the stipends by fixed numbers,
and told off men in companies of a thousand:
each group should have its leader, at whose judgment
the knights' undoubted courage might be tried,
and worthy honor shown to those thus tested;
so slackers might not claim rewards, nor wickedness
gleam under garb of virtue, nor the brave
lose recompense or fame for their bold deeds.
Among the ancient Macedonians
and under Philip, it had been the custom
to rouse the camp with trumpets, when the signal
was to be given; but the crash and din

of arms cut off the sound from reaching everyone.
Therefore by day a pole was to be raised,
at night a fire, or smoke, when camp was struck.
Lest any dare usurp the recompense
earned by another's bravery, ascribing
such deeds to his own strength, he ordered each
to content himself with action's just reward.
The brave he urged with prayer, with gold enticed
the mercenaries, and constrained with writs
the rank and file.
We read that Roman kings
set down the laws' appointed course for peoples
throughout the conquered world, when Jove above
and Emperor Theodosius on earth
had warded off the Furies' vengeance. Yet
it was by far a greater feat, to bind
men at arms through force of law, than fix
new ordinances for the vanquished; greater still
that soldiers should receive strict rules for war,
than that the laws prevail in time of peace.
[63] When all in time had willingly received
these edicts, when the citizens of Susa
had made over the town, and in its treasures
the troops were gladdened, the column turned in fury
towards the strongholds of the Uxii.
Medates ruled as prefect of the region,
a paragon of bravery and of troth.
He had no fear to suffer death for fealty,
and so endured as Darius' true friend.
Now from the natives Alexander learned
a covert route, by which the Greeks might gain
the city, unbeknown to its inhabitants.
He set Tauron, a man of proven merit,
over knights picked to go into such danger.
At dawn's first light, he moved to gain the narrows
by which the site's approaches were defended.
They cut down brush, with which they might construct
the wickerwork and shelters of a tortoise
against the fortress walls: so might armed youths

destroy the ramparts down to their foundations,
safe under the defenses of such effort.
But all access was hard, for there the ground
denied approach with menace of sharp stones,
and Alexander, battling harsh foes,
fought, too, the site itself, which living rock
had fortified; yet agile cohorts scaled
those narrow heights, their leader at their head.
[87] The tortoise set in place, no force, no prayer
could pull him back from the barbarian walls,
though from afar a hail of missiles rained
down upon his head; but first among
the vanguard, from beneath his crested helm
he thundered at the ramparts. Now he hurled
huge rocks, now dug with mattocks; now he thrust
a ram against the gates, now launched his missiles—
himself the engine of the world's sad fate.
And driving on his men, "For shame," he cried,
"for shame, my fellow victors over Asia!
To you have fallen all these cities, yet
you sleep beneath these wretched village walls.
What site, what wall might stand, what earthworks hold
before the Macedonians' hand? What ramparts,
what citadels could ever endure such force?
What stones, though laid on stable columns, may
resist, when that high wall feels the approach
of Alexander? Though it matched Olympus,
it topples, towers falling down before me."
[103] He'd spoken, and upon the highest citadel
Tauron appeared: the sight made bold the Greeks,
while fear and desperation gripped the citizens.
The hearts of some resolved to suffer all,
to lay their lives down for their native land,
while others would have fled, had they the chance.
Huge crowds took refuge in the cloud-swept stronghold.
Then thirty were dispatched to beg the victor
they might depart alive, but his response
was dire indeed: no room remained for pardon,
and scant delay for suffering or for grief.

The stricken townsmen languished in their fear,
meek in their dread of death. And so Medates
dispatched by night upon a hidden route
his prayers to Darius' mother, that she might
calm Alexander's wrath: so might he spare
in victory the vanquished and their city.
Medates knew the victor treated her
with honor due a mother. He himself
had wed her granddaughter, and in his veins
there flowed the blood of Darius' clan. And yet
she long refused his just entreaties, saying,
"Such pride ill suits the fortune I now suffer.
What countenance shall I wear in intercession,
captive before the victor? He who begs
more than he's due endures a just rebuke.
Hope without merit is no longer hope;
its true name is presumption. So I must
consider that I am a captive, not
recall I was a queen. Such bold entreaties
may tire, I fear, the king's flagging indulgence."
Yet Sisigambis felt the suppliants' grief,
and wrote to Alexander: should he not
desire to spare the vanquished, then at least
might he permit a conquered and repentant
Medates his own life? The moderation
and constant mercy that still marked the king
was seen in this one deed—that he forgave
Medates and them all, conceding to them
their prior liberty, and to the captives
gave back the captured city. He restored
ancestral fields to those who'd earlier tilled them,
to hold them henceforth without further tribute.
Had wavering Fortune given Darius
both town and victory with her own hand,
his mother's plea could have achieved no more
than foe bestowed upon the conquered foe.

[145] Immediately he made division of
the troops, and bade Parmenion go forth
to follow Darius on the level road,

while he himself retained his chosen knights.
His own course lay along the towering ridges
that ran unbroken into Persia's lands.
Here Alexander knew his gravest perils,
and here, as nowhere else, experience taught him
that fickle Fortune stands perpetually
for none upon the earth. He picked his route
through narrow passes where the road was lost,
through bends that brooked no press of mortal step.
The foe rushed down upon him from above,
and often forced him to retrace his path
with no scant loss of blood among him men.
Yet after all such dangers, gathering strength,
he broke the standards of the foe, and laid
their conquered arms beneath his own in triumph.
[161] Black night had scarce been scoured from the heavens,
when Alexander laid a bridge across
Araxes' waters, and rushed toward Persepolis,
which now he seized and left reduced to ashes.
That town, known for so many ancient kings,
surpassed by far the barbarous opulence
of all the cities, swollen with their wealth,
which he had taken earlier: there its kings
had brought all Persia's luxury. From its temples
were now drawn out the sacred gold, the heap
of ancient silver. From its shrines they seized
a mound of riches piled up by antiquity,
not for its use, so much as to attract
the wondering gaze of those who looked upon it.
They swiftly ran to plunder, and contention
arose among the thieves. Friends were cut down
in place of foes, less precious than the booty
they'd seized or found: those costly furnishings
were cause and cost of death. What each man seized,
he could no longer hold; his wickedness
prized only what he could retain no longer.
The purple garments of the kings were rent,
long labor of skilled craftsmen; golden vessels
encrusted with devices lay in shards,

and greed, content with nothing, left none whole.
So too the idols lay, their limbs wrenched off,
their beauty gone, a mutilated terror.
This was that city's end, which once had flowered
with titles of so many kings, which gave
so many lands her laws. Once, she had been
all Europe's lone and single terror, when
ten thousand keels obstructed all the deep
with her vast fleet, and she had dared immerse
the excavated hills in Neptune's waters,
and spread her sails upon the mountains' backs.
Kings after Alexander held the rest
of Persia's cities; but of this one you'll find
nowhere a trace, save that the swift Araxes
displays the leveled walls hard by its banks.

[196] You might pronounce the city worthy of
such wrack, or not. For Alexander, passing
towards its walls, had met a wretched sight,
three thousand captive Macedonians.
With bodies hewn, with lips, ears, hands, or feet
hacked off, shorn of their limbs, or robbed of sight,
or else diminished in some other member,
upon their foreheads barbarous signs were carved,
that such a notice might record their mockery.
At first, the king supposed they seemed not men
but effigies. But then he recognized them
and warmed with rising tears; that conquering army
wept, and triumph turned to sudden grief.
The king enjoined them in their misery
to keep their strength of mind, for he'd bestow
whatever they desired: they'd see again
Europe's sweet country, wives and dearest kin,
and in their fathers' soil they'd take their rest.
The wretched company withdrew behind
a palisade, until debate could settle
what they might best entreat. Some wished to stay
in Asian lands, while others deemed far sweeter
than foreign swards their own ancestral meadows.

[217] Euctemon, whose skilled tongue had made him famous,

thus spoke (so it's believed): "Just now it shamed us
to come forth from the darkness of the caves,
in which we were imprisoned, to seek aid;
and will you flaunt your bodies' demolition—
a cheerful sight!—before your countrymen,
your heads held high, though doubtful it remains
which conquers, grief or shame, amidst such fortune?
An unjust lot is better borne when hidden,
a bitter lot is better borne with tact
to hide one's wretched life. No land's so sweet,
so homely to the abject, as a strange one—
a dwelling without earlier fortune's witness.
A solitary place can bless the wretched,
when oblivion steals over earlier bliss.
Those who depend on hope and love of kin
forget how quickly streams of tears grow dry,
despite their soothing balm: lightly they come,
and lighter still recede. Those near the wretched
pay them their tears alone; when those are dry,
the love and pity of your kin will vanish.
The wretched's lot is lamentation; pride
belongs to happiness, and vaunting minds
know nothing of compassion. One who's shunned
was never truly prized; that love is true
which does not shun a friend in wretchedness.
But everyone, as soon as he considers
another's fortune, will recall his own,
and in that recollection quickly seek
outside himself what he has known within.
We, we ourselves, might shun each other's sight,
a mutual scandal, had a common fate
not doled an equal lot to all three thousand.
We took our tender wives in youth's first flush,
and then left them in scorn to don our arms.
With what a solemn gaze they'll welcome us—
our vile, lopped bodies shorn of Venus' tinder—
to their embrace, and how they'll long to share
the marriage-bed's delights! Is still their sex

so unfamiliar to us? Springtime breezes
are surer than a woman's heart, and adamant
is softer. Can she brook her wretched husband,
whom even in prosperity she chided?
Young men, I beg you—now your life is spent:
seek homes that suit your rough-hewn carcasses.
Lugubrious castaways, with one accord
let's seek fit dwellings. Unknown shores should hide us,
among those grown accustomed to our misery,
those who have ceased to cringe at our raw wounds."
[263] But when Euctemon finished, he was answered
by Theteus of Athens: "No one judges
his friend by mien of body; Fortune's mockery,
for all its harshness, sways no pious heart.
The brutal foe, and not creating Nature,
made us contemptible, and for my part,
I judge him worthy of all ills, who's shamed
by outcome of his fortune. Some are wont
to lay no hope in others' mercy, when
their darkest hours come on; but those same men
themselves would show none, were Fate's threads reversed.
The cruel of heart look inward, and suppose
that kindness rarely settles in men's minds.
You see the gods have offered more than prayer
could ever hope to gain—wives, country, children,
and our ancestral hearths. O may we thus
burst from our prison, to receive once more
the sight and air, the tongue and native ways
our fathers left us! Why will you remain here,
both wretch and slave, when you might gain your homeland,
where slavery, at least, can no more touch you?
For exiles who have suffered Fortune's all,
it's something still to lie down with one's fathers,
and bones entombed by kindred hands rest gentler.
Let others stay among the Persians, breathing
contentedly the Median air, if lack
of faith in sires and wives can tear them from
their own sweet fields. For me, I'll take the gift

the king bestows, and once again seek Europe
and native soil, now that the gods have offered
the free sight of the country of my birth."
[290] So Theteus concluded. But he found
few shared in his intent, and custom's force,
more powerful than nature, won the hearts
of his companions. Concurring with their plan,
the Great One in his generosity
shared out not only fields of fertile richness,
but money for supplies, and varied flocks,
and heaps of burgeoning grain: so might the soil
not lack its increase, nor its farmers coin.
[297] When he'd provided for them with such wisdom,
his troops restored, Mars' hero entered Media
in headlong rush to track the steps of Darius.
Swifter than a leopard he pursued,
lest flight should snatch from him the king of Persia,
who still remained his triumph's greatest portion.
But Belus' son now came to Ecbatan,
the capital of Media; he'd resolved
to pass on thence to Bactria. Meanwhile, Rumor
announced that Alexander was at hand,
against whose army's wingèd pace no distance
seemed wide enough between them. Darius' heart
was changed, as was his counsel: now preparing
his arms for war, he chose to die in combat,
a course more honorable than to prolong
a life so often battered by the Fates.
[311] And so he bade his comrades pause a while,
and, gazing on them, said, "If similar toils
had joined me to base men, who deemed what death
soever to be honorable, then rather
would I pass over silently those matters
that should be spoken, than consume this time
in words of vanity. But I have tried the strength
of your virtue, which displays more loyalty
than I could wish, or than befits full honor.
I've learned how venerable is friendship's name,
how genuine faith is kept by genuine friends.

Such deeds oblige me to presume I'm worthy
of such companions. You alone remain,
Persia's one glory, of so many soldiers.
Twice have you followed me in flight, twice followed
your vanquished prince's arms. Your loyalty
and constancy, which prove your mind unshaken,
remove my dread to trust I'm yet a king,
and still does Persia dare confess I reign.
You worthies, as I judge, who've rather chosen
to hold the vanquished camp, than to pursue
the ensigns of the victor, to whom God,
if I cannot, will pay on my behalf
due thanks on high—for never shall posterity
be so forgetful of the right, so deaf
and unobliged to justice, that it will not
extol you to the skies with your fair praise,
and tell your memorable deeds, or not commend
you and your merit—after death the buried
will live in fame, for virtue uneclipsed
alone cheats death. So I rely upon
my men's strong counsel and courageous spirit,
and even if I might plot hidden flight—
which ever I abhor—yet would I now
go forth to meet the foe. In his own realm
though Darius is an exile, yet how long,
O citizens, will you endure as king
of your ancestral realm a foreign ruler?
My lot shall be to lose my life with honor,
or else to scourge the foe and take my cities
once more, regaining swiftly what we've lost.
Or would you deem it proper I should wait,
vanquished, upon the judgment of the victor?
Shall Darius sue for power in one region,
as did Mazaeus? Shall I be preserved
for such disgrace, who held all Asia's reins,
and rule—the victor's boast—by his largesse?
Ever shall it be unfit, that anyone
should take away this honor due my head,
or boast that he's restored what he had taken.

I'll lose my empire while I live; indeed,
I'll lose my crown and life on the same day.
A costly death will strip off Darius' crown,
and strip away his life in that same hour.
If such is your courageous mind as well,
O comrades, none will be compelled to suffer
the Greeks' unspeakable and haughty pride,
once Fate has struck. Each man's right hand will be
his own end, or else evil's fitting punishment.
If, then, the gods above desert those who
fight wars of justice; if they deem it crime
to make upright defense—at least the end
will come with honor, and still may the brave
die a distinguished death. By all the deeds
our ancestors performed, I pray you now,
by princely praise once paid our fathers, by
the illustrious men to whom so many times
the Macedonians, a subject race,
surrendered tribute, I beseech you, comrades—
take courage worthy of your stock, and may
Olympus witness your defeat or victory,
the one or other bred of glorious battle."

[370] Arsamus' scion finished, but the troops
did not receive those words in his same spirit.
The shouts of approbation due the sayings
of speakers who incite emboldened crowds
were lacking there. Raw fear hedged every brow,
till Artabazus, chief of the king's friends,
broke through the silence: "With one mind," he said,
"we'll follow the king's arms; the end that claims
you and our country shall claim us as well."
The rest received his words with glad assent
and raised a raucous tumult—as upon
the Aegean Sea, a sailor without hope
will cheer his lifeless comrades, though the South Wind
plots against him, when the stern's been shattered:
dissembling fear, he strengthens trembling hearts,
and makes to cross the deep in adverse wind.

[384] But Bessus now perpended dire outrage:

he and Narbazanes had laid the plan,
backed up by no few troops, to set their hands
upon the king while yet he lived, and thus
to garner easy favor from the victor,
should Alexander overtake them; but
if Fate should let them slip his speeding ranks,
they'd dare to kill their king, to take the throne
and join the fray anew, their strength restored.
And so Narbazanes seized on a moment
well suited to his crime: "O king," he said,
"I know my words will please you little, nor
their burden find your heart a welcome haven.
But gravest wounds are healed by fiercest iron,
and bitter is the medicine for pain.
A dire potion cures severe diseases,
and sailors, fearing shipwreck, with some discard
save what they can, by loss redeeming loss.
You know some hostile god impedes your battles;
a hostile Chance still presses back your Persians.
We need new omens: Fortune must be tried
all ways we can. Good king, for some brief interval,
lay off the kingdom's pomp. Grant to another
the empire's highest governance, that he
may hold the name and omen of a king,
till Mars shall cease his storm. The foe cast out
from Asia's lands, to you, its rightful king,
he will restore the realm. For such a deed
the time of expectation shall be brief:
still greater strength remains, more might in war,
among the Bactrian and Indian peoples
than was exhausted by our earlier battles.
Why do we rush into calamity
like sheep astray? Brave minds hold death in scorn;
yet men do not despise their lives, but love them.
The base and those who weary of their toil
may come to view their life as something vile—
what marvel, that the struggle of the living
should seem like death to knaves? But nothing's left
untried by arduous virtue in its bravery:

it moves all things, all things attempts, advancing
toward death as last recourse, when nothing else
seems to remain, and destiny's played out.
Therefore, O king, commit for now to Bessus,
whom occasion offers, your realm's governance,
that, at the proper time, he may restore
to you the sceptre and the empire's throne."

[425] Their lord's good will and patience scarce restrained him
when such a speech was ended. "Now I know,"
he said, "cruel serf, you've found the funest hour
wherein you'll work harsh outrage on your master,
and break, though still a slave, the Fates' slim thread."
Thus speaking, with drawn sword he would have slain him,
had Bessus not with suppliant countenance
besought the king: the traitor wore a guise
of indignation, and around him stood
his throng of followers; he would have bound him
at once, had he not sheathed his naked blade.

[435] They ordered then their men to lay a camp
sequestered from the rest; but Artabazus
advised the king to spare his wrath, and treat
the moment by its own necessity.
"Endure the foolish error of your men
with equanimity," he said, "for Alexander
approaches, swift and strong of arms. You must
keep hold upon your army with mild love,
lest discord turn aside their loyal sentiments,
and Bactria withdraw its soldiers from you."

[443] Arsamus' scion obeyed, and pitched his tents
as gods and Fate required. Despair and grief,
close comrades of the vanquished, cast their shadow
upon his spirits. In the ungoverned camp
diverse thoughts moved men's hearts. At hand now stood
the day of the king's doom, nor did he shoulder
the kingdom's burden as he'd done before,
but solitary kept the royal tents,
and turned his watchful cares within his breast.

[451] But now those two considered what they'd planned—
an outrage born of lust for royal power.

They recognized the king could not be seized
without great effort, for no little fear
and reverence for kings reigns with the Persians.
The royal majesty carries great weight;
the very name of king shakes barbarous hearts
among that race. Those whom barbarity
feared amidst success, it still reveres
though gods now press them down. In adverse chance,
the veneration of their past lives on,
and, once shown honor, they are paid it ever.
Such loyalty and grace towards a king
obtained among that race, that open force
would not allow the criminals to bind
their lord without a slaughter of their followers.
So, settling on deceit, they begged his pardon
for prior madness: with dissembling voice,
they claimed they'd now return, and that the weight
of guilt oppressed them duly; again they stood
prepared to suffer death for the king's sake.
[468] The morrow's Titan brought to light again
a world lost in the blackness of the night,
and Darius gave the signal to strike camp.
The sharers of the crime stood near at hand
among their many soldiers, shrewdly offering
their solemn offices, the outward mien
of those who'd follow the king's might. But outrage,
the shamelessness of such a crime, lay hidden
deep in their minds. Still Darius shone forth
atop his lofty car, and still he wielded
the gleaming sceptre and the realm's insignia.
The treasonous band lay suppliant on the ground,
and sued for pardon; the traitor undertook
to venerate his duke, though soon a slave
would drag him off in chains. So he compelled
the son of Belus, amidst flowing tears,
his face grown stiff with weeping, to believe him.
Not even then did crime grieve treachery's fellows,
when both beheld how mild his nature was—
their king and fellow man—whom they deceived.

Secure, thus, and unwary of the hour
then at hand, which chance and those two slaves
had prepared, he sought now to evade
the hordes of Alexander and the Greeks—
whom alone he feared! With loosened reins
he spurred his flight and hastened toward far lands.

[490] But Patron, leader of the Grecian cohort,
pure in his life and stable in his loyalty,
an unfeigned friend of Darius, discovered
the parricidal fraud. A thousand of
his men in arms marched with him handsomely,
as he approached the king and gained the chance
to speak with him. "O best of kings," he said,
"Narbazanes and Bessus now make ready
with bloody sword to trip their snare upon you.
This day will end your life, or theirs. Permit us
to guard your person. Order that your tents
be pitched among us, as the affair demands.
We've left Europe behind, and neither Bactria
nor India is ours: in you alone
we lay our hopes; you are our fields and hearths.
A foreigner who fled to you, I'd never
seek to become the surety of your welfare,
if I saw any other who might do so."
The glory of a king's near-preservation
marked Patron's excellence. But if any read
these deeds, if any read our song, then never
shall France's generations cease to tell
of Patron, who, enduring with the poet,
shall live undying through all time to come.

[511] Now I declare that by no accident
the ages run, but they are linked eternally
with well-knit cause. Let none suppose that chance
fortuitously steers this world's events.
Things turn according to the law their maker
set from eternity. Though Darius
could have survived by heeding Patron's counsel,
he followed Fate's decree, and so replied,

"I know and oft have tried your faithfulness,
but never shall I leave my native race,
nor seek to separate myself from those
whom I've esteemed so often. Better that
I am deceived, than that I should condemn them.
Whatever Fortune bids, I'll sooner suffer
among them, than be thought a fleeing traitor.
If my own men do not desire my safety,
too late I perish; death I freely choose."
[525] The king's decision left Patron amazed
and driven to despair. He turned, distracted,
back to the Grecian cohort, still prepared
to suffer all things with the loyalty
and upright rigor of the just. But Bessus,
though ignorant of the Hellenic tongue,
still recognized the greatness of his turmoil,
and, through interpreters, the parricide
learned what his words had meant. Now Darius
he would have slain, if he had not supposed
he might bring him alive to Alexander.
By such a plan, those partners in the slaughter
hoped they could win some favor of the victor.
Therefore they left their crime till night's fit hour—
night's hour, when deeds of foulness are performed;
night's hour, when those things please and go unpunished
that by daylight brought shame; when fear grows bold,
and guilty brows can't blush. Then Bessus strove
falsely to honor Darius and to thank him,
that with his decorous and pleasing speech
he'd shunned the faithless words of treacherous hirelings:
"His eye on wealth alone, with the king's head
he'd please the Macedonian tyrant, and
would soon have handed him that mortal gift.
No wonder—for it's clear a venal mercenary,
bought for a price, will set a price on all.
An exiled pauper, having neither child,
nor home, nor wife, will sway as does a reed
for price of purchased goods." Arsamus' scion

nodded assent; and yet, he knew the Greeks
had brought a true report. But to this pass
all things had come, two choices equally cruel,
and full of fear, and hopeless: not to entrust
himself to his own men and pay them heed,
or lay his head before their swords' deception.

Book Seven

The Headings of the Seventh Book

The seventh book arms slaves against their master,
shows forth his justice, casts him into chains.
The Great One follows Darius, and in battle
subdues the routed minions of such crime.
Then, pierced by javelins, Darius at last
commits his final words, on point of death,
to Polistratus, come to seek fresh water.
The Greek king laves his corpse with copious tears,
and buries him. Again the tumult presses
commons and lords; against the foe he rages.

Book Seven

The evening star stood motionless, and Phoebus,
his horses curbed, clung to the shore in grief.
Latona's virgin daughter checked her light
and hesitated to display her countenance,
slowing the reins of coming night in sadness.
But holy universal Love, that law
which binds all things in one eternal knot
and rules the whole, rebuked them both, and bade them
fulfill their given duties. Thetis' waves
now foamed and eddied as the day sank under them,
and with the sun men's labor sought its rest.
Yet torment still awaited grieving Darius,

who stood upon the evening of his life,
to make his own end at the world's dark twilight.
Wretched, alone, he shut his tent, and pondered
what course lay open to him. But the counsels
of hapless men, whose lives misfortune compasses,
are ever filled with weakness and despair.
[17] Yet thus he spoke: "Cursed father of the gods,
into what straits do you now draw me? For
what sin does Fate's blind cast dispose my ruin?
Spirits above, what crime deserves such penalties,
that neither friend nor kin leaves me a place
where safely I might shed fear for my life?
More savagely than any open enemy,
a foe within my house thirsts for my soul,
and holds the knife against an old man's throat.
If Darius was crowned unworthily
with such a diadem, or gained unrighteously
the sway of all of Asia; if I ruled
my subjects badly; if I played the tyrant,
attempting to undo my fathers' laws,
or overturning common rights; if tyranny
oppressed my citizens by force of arms;
if as a wicked judge at the tribunal
I turned a deaf ear to the poor man's case;
if bribes swayed my corrupted judgment, or
I sold fair justice for vile, fatal lucre;
if sons bewail their losses, disinherited
of their ancestral vineyards by my agency;
if, hating faith and right, I've coursed the world
with impure mind—then now I merit death,
nor do I beg one hour of Fate's reprieve.
Your gift, O gods, has granted life enough.
Unleash the Furies, let Narbazanes
and Bessus rage against me; let my blood,
now cold with age, drench all my house, and thus
sate heaven's righteous anger. But if justice
has flourished under my protection, if
I kept the laws, and followed reason's dictates—
as nature and the wanton flesh permitted—

then take the servant's blade from his lord's throat.
Let Darius prosper for his guiltless life,
and death be turned upon those who deserve it.
May innocence allow just men to prosper,
and may I live while guilt consumes the wicked.
Or if the gods' high will remains unshaken,
if Fate's unwavering course shall still my breath,
and Atropos hastens to break her thread,
cutting short my life—why should it be given
to other hands and not to mine? And why
should I escape the Argives, only to fall
as victim to Narbazanes? Does not
my blood remain, my right hand, and my sword?
Why hesitate to free my life from Fate?"
[59] He would have pierced his entrails with cold steel,
save that the eunuch who alone stood by him
alarmed the encampment's tents with lamentation.
Then others, breaking forth in tears, announced
the king had fallen. Barbarous wailing rose
throughout the camp, and stricken by the din
the countryside resounded, while the ether
was shaken overhead. His men dared not
take up their arms: they feared the henchmen's swords.
Though piety and faith both urged the Persians
to arm themselves, lest wickedly they seem
to leave their lord abandoned, still their terror
decided matters, and strong fear of death
prevailed to shut out honor's clear command.
[70] Lo! Rushing through the astonished Persian ranks,
the partners in the sacrilege came marching,
and broke a path with swords through those who'd gathered;
they bound the king, whom they'd thought dead already.
What excesses of Fate, the fickle toss
that settles human outcomes! He who previously
had sat astride a gilded car, and made
his subjects tremble, now sat bound of hand,
no longer master of himself, upon
a narrow seat atop a meagre wain.
Yet, that at least the name of king be honored,

the slave, more vicious than a serpent, ordered
his master to be bound in golden fetters.
The royal household was seized like spoils of war,
and though the weight of coins pressed down the chariots,
those burdened with the gains of darkest evil
prepared for flight. Infamy of all the East,
you ministers of crime and high deceit,
where will you go, what land, pray, will endure you?
What lord's secure whose slave thirsts for his blood?
[91] Meanwhile, his army girt for high endeavor,
the conqueror of lands rushed on his course
to trace the steps of Darius. Preparing
a siege around the walls of Ecbatan,
he'd take the fugitive king, and raze the city
down to its cornerstones by force of arms,
and set his hand to long wars' final strife.
But when he heard that Darius, bent on flight,
had moved to quit the city, then at once
he turned his course and left the fields of Persia,
spurred by his valor and bent on giving chase.
Since rumor's breeze noised it abroad that Darius
was passing into Media, thence to Bactria,
there he prepared to follow. But a messenger
turned him again, declaring that the king
now lay enchained: he narrated the sequence
of all events in seemly, well-joined order.
[106] The Macedonian shuddered at such news,
and, summoning his dukes, addressed them thus:
"Brief is the labor, comrades, that remains,
and great are its rewards. Not far from here
have Darius' men abandoned him; he waits
for Fortune's ills and evil's final limit.
Perhaps he has already met his fate,
or else still lives against his will. Therefore
we'll goad our sluggish mounts with doubled speed,
plunging our steps towards the enemy,
to offer life to our afflicted foe.
It is no less a victory, to spare
one who now stands broken in misery,

than to break him who yet remains rebellious."
The princes cheered the king's words, surging forward
to promise their support through gravest peril.
And so the fatal scourge of all the world
set out before his ranks. No rest by night
relieved the labor of the day with sleep.
Thus on the Giants fell the wrath of Jove,
who, poets feign, armed his right hand with lightning:
then, when Typhoeus with his hundred hands
stretched forth his knotted arms against the heavens,
you might have seen Mars blazing forth, or Pallas
showing upon her shield the visage serpentine,
or Phoebus scattering darts with fatal bow.

[128] They came, when stars were just appearing, to
the town where Bessus, maddened in his heart,
had bound his lord. Two men approached, who loathed
the monstrous outrage, and to the company
of parricides preferred the safety found
among the Macedonians. These men
led Alexander by a shorter route,
while Phoebus slumbered. Marching in squared columns,
they checked their course, so that the trailing cohorts
could close ranks with the vanguard. Now the Delian
was equidistant from his two abodes,
when lo! the refugee Brocubelus
reported to the king that Darius lived,
and now was but two hundred stades away.
"But see to it," he said, "your army marches
in close-kept ranks, and does not stumble weaponless
upon the armed lines. Outrage arms the parricides
more harshly for the slaughter, since despair
proclaims your heart holds no room for forgiveness."

[145] On hearing his advice, the princes' zeal
blazed forth, and Alexander's eagerness
to track the slaves' encampment grew yet stronger.
They loosed the reins upon their worn-out steeds,
who flew on wings grown under doubled goads.
The Greeks soon heard the din and crash of wheels,
and foe could have spied foe, had not the dust

blocked off their gaze in horrid, roiling clouds.
Then Alexander bade the Greeks hold back,
until the dust storm ceased, and they could see
the hostile throngs. Then Bessus turned his gaze,
and, as the dust subsided, from the mountain's
lofty peak saw them advancing breathlessly;
their armor flashed with light against dark iron.
He shuddered at the sight, and frigid hearts
trembled in knowledge of their monstrous guilt.
Across the gap, the Macedonian nation
saw Bessus, and struck out along the heights
in eagerness to meet the enemy,
despite their unmatched forces—for if Bessus
had possessed such courage, strength, and stores
for battle, as for crime, if martial vigor
had matched his force in outrage and in treason,
he could have beaten back Pellaeus' strength,
avenging Asia on the Macedonians.
Indeed, the barbarous troops who thronged his camp
outstripped the Greeks in strength, as in their numbers:
restored as they had been by sleep and food,
they could have taught their long-exhausted enemy
that rest confers much strength upon an army.
    [175] But terror of the Macedonians
and Alexander's formidable name—
no small advantage in the fray—turned hearts
to trembling and to doubt that they could conquer.
The treacherous cohort fled, their arms in rout,
backs turned toward chests, degenerate in their flight.
The sharers in that crime not to be spoken
then girded up their hearts for the last outrage.
Insistently they urged on Darius
to leave his car and quickly mount a horse,
and move to save his life by flight. But spurning
such venomous advice, with flowing tears
he called to witness the avenging gods,
and begged them for fierce Alexander's faithfulness;
he vowed he'd not accompany crime's minions.
"No fear of death," he said, "or stroke of Fate

will force the king to join the camp of criminals.
The blade of Fortune holds no new disaster.
The death that now the parricide is threatening
will be the antidote of sorrow; death's stark potion
will heal me of all labor and all care."

[195] Bile rose within their hearts at his response.
With bloody lance they pierced their lord and father,
casting their darts upon him like hail-showers,
then leaving him at last, spattered with gore,
and gashed upon the breast with many wounds.
Lest they should follow after the deserters,
they hacked the team yoked to the royal car
with swords and javelins, and the same end
met the two servants who'd accompanied
the king in life, and now shared in his death.
To hide the trace of such a monstrous act,
they then took separate paths: Bessus made haste
for Bactria; Narbazanes would seek
Hyrcania's groves. The others scattered, fleeing,
some urged by fear, some clinging still to hope,
best of companions amidst doubtful things.
Only five hundred men remained, who chose
to stand against the Macedonian ranks,
and die for justice and the honor of
their fallen land—perhaps because they hoped
to lengthen life by strength of arms, perhaps
because it shamed them to survive their king.

[215] But while with rushing speech the barbarous legion
debated whether they should turn their backs,
although the foe was near, or face the Greeks,
lo! on the wings of swift, triumphant courage
the Macedonian band swept down upon them,
all arms and force and fury of red Mars.
The din and rack of warfare burst once more
upon them, and the fearful gained by flight
no more than did the brave man by his boldness:
the brave were slain, the fearful taken captive;
and though the wonder merits disbelief,
the captives numbered more than those who took them,

and in its weight the booty far exceeded
the number of the plunderers. The rebels
fell nonetheless with no small share of praise,
three thousand noble men who stood against them.
Neither the rage of death nor slaughter's rancor
grew still until those young men sworn to bloodshed
were held back by a sign from Alexander
to check the fury of their murderous swords.
Then like a herd of beasts those who survived
were driven forth; yet in the entire column
was none to show the Greeks a trace of Darius.

[235] They searched the Persian wagons one by one,
but never found the corpse, that fatal outrage:
upon a far-off path deep in a valley
lay the king's beasts, pierced through the breast with darts,
lamenting their own death, and that of Darius.
Nearby, a chattering stream fell with loud prattle,
and held its place amidst the vernal grass.
Its parent was a spring that flowed forth pure
through rocky depths, and thence dripped from the bank;
it moistened the dry turf with its sweet nectar.
Here Polistratus, spent after the battle,
exhausted by tempestuous thirst, was drawn
to ease his parched throat in the river's flow.
He saw the wounded beasts and car of Darius,
concealed by cast-off hides; saw, too, the king
who even now was breathing out his life.

[250] And drawing near to look, he soon discovered
the wounded, wild-eyed Darius, who lay
upon the boundary of his life and death.
The king rejoiced to hear the other ask
his name in Indic speech, and thus he answered,
as far as one could hear his failing voice:
"One solace only comforts Darius
in present fortune and in coming death,
that with you I have no need of interpreter,
but speak my last to comprehending ears,
nor will my final words flow forth in vain.
How welcome now would be the presence of

the Macedonian king, that such a foe
might hear me in his piety, and I
might mingle words with him in conversation.
One fleeting hour might settle ancient quarrels.
But since the Fates deny me his own presence,
receive these words, whoever you may be,
and carry them to Alexander: after
so many struggles, in his debt I die,
beholden to him that in moderation,
forgetting hostile wrath, his clement heart
received my mother and my children kindly:
he showed no tyrant's hostile spirit to
the vanquished, but a regal mind more faithful
to me, his foe, than did my kin and subjects.
Those near me seized my life, to whom I'd given
both life and realms. How wretched to relate it!
Among my foes I stand in safety, only
to fall among my friends, slain by those men
in whose protection I should have found security.
To these men may a just prince dole the recompense
that parricide deserves—as I'd have paid it,
had Fortune given me the victory.
For in this crisis, more than my own lot
hangs in the scales: the cause of all who rule
the masses, and control a nation's reins
in me is put to judgment. Let the Great One
decide with even hand what punishment
awaits such guilt, what vengeance expiates
a sin of such outrage. But if he tarries,
or acts perchance with less than righteous vigor,
the king's repute will change from what it's been;
his lustrous image will grow tarnished for it.
A pious king, what's more, must take precautions
against a like plague, and avoid the dangers
of sudden chance. Here justice, there utility
is weighed: let him keep both with equal vigor.
One thing I pray for with my dying pleas
before infernal Chaos and the gods:
may all the conquered world serve Alexander,

according to the sequence of the Fates;
upon the mighty earth may he reign mightiest,
and may the king not grudge that I receive
the final honors of a rightful burial."
He spoke, and stretched out his right hand, as though
its token should be sent to Alexander.
A lethal sleep crept through his stiffening limbs,
and, breaking from its bonds of clay at last,
shunning the wretched hospice of the flesh,
the sacred spirit burst free in the breeze.
    [306] O happy souls, if, while life's warmth suffuses
the quickened limbs, they gain a foretaste of
the respite and rewards that righteous shades
receive when life has passed, and of the contraries
the wicked may expect! The love of gain
in all its deadliness would not ensnare them,
nor lust, the ally of the flesh, consume
their inward parts. At lavishly set tables
the obscene belly of the son would not
devour his father's fields; nor would Bacchus
pant in his close confinement; nor would Liber
strain horribly to break the iron-bound casks
in which he is imprisoned. Simon's heirs
would not affect the honor of a see
bought for a price; the bishop's sacred chair
would know no taint of evil Lucre's goad.
No beardless boy, however bright his ancestry,
would set his sights upon a bishop's greatness,
until his age and character and learning
had gained him an election—and no matter
what excellence of lineage spoke for him.
The fathers who derive their name *a cardine*
would not be led by malice to create
two lords over the world. The smell of money
would not hold sway, the bribed judge would not twist
the shape of judgment. Neither would two lands
at equal distance over narrow straits
mourn for their bishops, slain without respect
for holy office. But because the flesh

is led astray by lust for fleeting things,
and hastens after momentary goods,
it snares the soul with this world's brief enticements,
and blots the memory of its beginning,
the knowledge of Whose image gave it birth,
and of the end to which the flesh must come.
Thus ignorance of the true Good prevails;
so is it that we scorn fair Reason's bridle,
and long for what Nature forbids, and man,
prepared for every crime, shows no respect
for that to which right and the law give reverence.
So was it that Bessus, enflamed with love
of power, feared no man, cared for no gods,
but cut his lord and father's fatal thread.
Yet you, O Darius, if what we write
will someday merit credence—rightfully
will France equate your praise with that of Pompey.
Surviving with your poet still, your glory
will live undying through all times to come.

[348] The Great One, when he'd heard of Darius' passing,
hastened his course with restless mind, and washed
the corpse with tears that flowed forth in a stream.
Laying aside a prince's mien, he sat
wringing his hands and grieving for the slain man,
whom he had tried so often to cast down
while still he stood. Drying his tears, and cleansing
his face with royal purple, now he spoke:
"There is one solace left to wretched mortals,
that glory knows no death, and reputation
meets no decline. If reputation's glory
matches the merits of your life, O Darius,
King of the Persians, hoary length of time
will never sully word of your achievements,
nor will the file of time rub out your worth.
The entire earth will read that you dared stand,
forever bright with praise, against the Fates,
opposing Macedonian Alexander.
If Fate with better omen had preserved you
alive on my behalf, you'd have discovered

nothing is lighter than the Grecian yoke.
A lesser king than one alone, received
into a share of empire by the Great One,
you would have given laws to other men.
Would that the slavish band had left it to me
to gain praise for my clemency in victory
towards the vanquished foe; but since their swords
cut short their father's lengthened thread, at least
you'll be avenged by one who while you lived
stood as your foe. So may it fall to me,
when I've subdued the Orient in battle,
to pierce the shores of the Hesperides,
and send a threatening fleet against the West,
turning again to bow the necks of Gaul
beneath the sway of Greece. So may the gods
grant that I cross the Alps and break the might
of Rome, and of the people of Liguria."
[379] He spoke, and, having paid the wonted obsequies,
buried with kingly care that regal body.
He ordered the embalmed corpse laid to rest
in Darius' ancestral tombs, and there
a lofty pyramid was later raised,
which that Appelles wroghte subtilly
with snowy marble facings. Molten metal
was poured into the cracks, to join the stones
in mutual love inside the monument.
Where each joint was exposed, gold gleamed; engraved
with varied images, its light flashed forth.
The weight lay on four equidistant columns,
whose base was bronze, whose shafts rose up in silver,
while at their summit, capitals of gold
had been drawn out of twice-refining fires.
[393] Above these rose—such was Apelles' craft—
clearer than glass, purer than placid streams,
a crystal image of the turning sky,
a hollow shell of balanced weight, on which
the tripart world lay beautifully described.
Here Asia's seat was broadly spread, while there
her sisters each received a lesser space.
Here, by clear symbols, places were distinguished—

rivers, peoples, cities, forests, mountains,
provinces and towns, and every island
hemmed in by surging seas. What every land
was rich in, what it lacked, was there inscribed:
Libya is fruitful. Near the Syrtes
Ammon begs for showers. Nile's stream
enriches Egypt. India is endowed
with ivory and with shores decked out in gems.
Great Carthage with its lofty citadels
marks Africa, and the immortal fame
of Athens picks out Greece. The Palatine
makes Rome proud in her growth. Sabaea glories
in incense, Spain in Herculean Gades,
France in her soldiery, Campania
in wide-famed wine, the Britons in their Arthur,
and Normandy in customary arrogance.
England entices. Love of possession burns
Liguria. The Teuton vents his rage.
Around the outer edges of that dome,
the sliding Ocean roamed. Between the lands,
dividing Asia from the other two,
there lay the sea—the Sea, toward which descend
all vagrant rivers in their twisting banks:
by circling routes they plunge into the deep.
[421] And since Apelles was not ignorant
of Daniel's meaning, with this epigram
he marked the stones:
HERE LIES THE FIGURED RAM
WHOSE DOUBLE HORNS GREAT ALEXANDER BROKE
HAMMER OF ALL THE WORLD
Then, following
the Hebrews and their Scriptures, he set down
the years of humankind from its creation,
how all the sequence of past times revolved
until the warlike Great One's victories.
The sum of years were read thus: twice two thousand,
four hundred twice, six tens, and still twice four.
[431] The Macedonian that same while summoned
his troops to take the gifts of their deserving.
He healed their wounds and groans with huge rewards,

and at the suited time set out a banquet
for all the camp, restoring them with wine.
But while the army held the cups at leisure,
a sudden rumor stirred their ranks—such failings
will often mark a host left to its idleness.
They heard that Alexander, flushed with victory,
now that the foe was tamed and Persia conquered,
would seek again the sweet realms of their country.
Crazed to return, though none confirmed the rumor,
they ran like madmen through the camp's far quarters.
They packed the tents in wagons, wrapped their gear
and stowed the cooking pots, as though the march
were set for the next morning. Shouts of gladness
rose through the camp, and mingled with the stars.

[448] When the unconquered prince had heard the rumor,
his soul froze in astonished, secret terror,
and fury seized the slackened reins of reason.
But when his mind returned, and checked his rage,
he called his dukes and tearfully lamented:
in mid-course would the common rank and file
snatch all the world from him; upon the threshold
of glory, power over all the earth
would be withheld from Alexander. Nothing
would he bear back but shame into his homeland,
the fortune of the vanquished, not the victor.
The envy of the gods blocked such endeavors—
the gods, who draw brave hearts with sweet enticements
of love for native soil. Now nameless men
of no distinction wanted to return
to their ancestral lands; if they but tarried,
great praise would mark their path. The courtiers lauded
the king's words, and they pledged him all their strength;
they claimed the princes and the commoners
would follow his commands in every danger,
if only he would offer flattery
to soothe the ears of those who hesitated.

[467] And so the dukes were summoned to a council.
Then, while the crowd looked on, before the princes
Alexander spoke: "O friends, no wonder,

when you recall your deeds in all their honor,
that you should turn your minds to thoughts of home,
where fame chants the distinction of your labors,
and shining glory raises up your exploits.
You've freed your homeland of its Persian bondage;
Phoenicia, Persia, Media, Syria,
Armenia—your arm subdued them all.
Beneath your yoke lie Lydia, Cappadocia,
the Parthians, and the mountains of Cilicia.
Your toughness won for me more lands than chance
has given cities to earth's other kings.
If, by eternal treaty, the possession
of all these lands I've conquered with swift prowess
remained certain and fixed, O citizens,
I'd choose to strike out for my native cities
and for my own sweet land, though you restrained me.
There might I see my mother and two sisters,
and claim that praise I've won along with you.
But no firm root holds our new empire steady,
and victory's still doubtful, while barbarians
take up the yoke with less than full submission.
And so there's need of short delay, until
those savage hearts grow soft in their due season,
and foreign minds lay down their own long habits.
Fruits mature with time; harsh vintages
mellow in season, lacking understanding.
The long day tames the maddened souls of beasts
beyond the wont of nature. Human masters
soothe fierce and untamed lions by their gestures.
You've conquered Persia, but you've not subdued her,
for those restrained by arms, not law of character,
who fear their masters face to face, will prove
their foes when they depart. Though Persia's prince
is dead, there still remains an unchecked foe.
Bessus the parricide and his Narbazanes
still hold the kingdom and go forth to battle.
What shame, that slaves should grasp with bloody hand
a sceptre won by virtue of that outrage,
though they were born to service! Just as doctors

cut noxious growths from bodies long afflicted,
so I, too, judge that we should leave behind us
nothing that bars the path, but cut away
whatever might endanger realms we quit.
The spark from some small lamp, if it's neglected,
can often prove the cause of greater ruin.
The quarter where your foe remains secure
leaves you the less secure. The foe you scorn
becomes the braver and the stronger for it.
[516] "Have we then conquered Darius, to leave
his empire to Bessus the parricide?
Lords of all lands, put this great shame far from you.
The work is short, and short the road. A journey
of but four days remains: the parricide
can hope thereafter only for swift death.
You've crossed so many streams, so many passes,
crossed over gorges, over hideous lakes,
made roads through rocks in unnamed, trackless places.
No sea now roils before us, but all things
offer a smooth and even road to triumph.
Just on the threshold lies the victor's palm.
Few remain to be conquered. Endless glory
will clothe your memory, when generations
hear credulously of the penalties
slaves paid who killed their lord. A worthy labor,
that none escaped your hands whom reputation
accuses of their father's murder. By
this one deed, soldiers, you'll sustain your honor
forever, and gain Asia's gratitude."
He'd spoken, and they all raised up their hands,
in pledge that they would follow through all dangers,
whatever battles were to come. As one,
young men and old cried out their joy and gladness.
And so the Great One bade his eager men
strike camp, and swiftly raged against his foe.

Book Eight

The Headings of the Eighth Book

The eighth book tames Hyrcania, and presents
the Amazon in arms; she seeks what's fair.
Greek wealth's devoured by flames—a wondrous deed.
The crime of Dimus is disclosed. There follow
Philotas' awful groans, his speech and death.
Bessus, the wicked and implacable,
captured, is hanged, and lays his father's shade.
The Great One attacks Scythia. A messenger
does nothing by his speech to bend his wrath.
A race before unconquered is subdued.

Book Eight

Lamenting Memnon's death with endless grief,
three times the Dawn had strewn her radiant beams
through all the earth, when earth's sole conqueror,
valiant and swiftly lunging toward all peril,
approached Hyrcania's boundaries with his host.
He'd scarcely gained the victory, or heard
the supplications of the lisping Bagoas
to grant bloodstained Narbazanes his life,
when Queen Talestris of the Amazons,
aflame with her desire to see the king,
approached the camp with virgin retinue.
All peoples dwelling from the Caucasus

to rushing Phasis' wide-encircling stream
received this woman's laws. When once an audience
was granted to her with the king, she swiftly
descended from her horse, with quiver slung
from her left arm, two spear shafts in her right.
(The dress of Amazons does not obscure
their bodies wholly. On the left, their chests
are bared; their garments settle on the rest,
and hide what must be hidden, though the soft
raiment doesn't fall below the knee-joint.
The left teat is preserved until adulthood
to nurse their infants of the female sex;
the other one receives an early searing
to ease their wielding of the pliant bow,
and leave them unencumbered for the javelin.)

[24] Perusing, then, the king with wary eye,
Talestris marveled that his meagre body
ill fit his fame, and silently she pondered
where the great virtue of the unvanquished prince
might lie concealed: the simple savage mind
respects and judges all according to
their bodies' beauty and their splendid raiment,
and thinks none capable of mighty deeds,
save those whom nature has seen fit to bless
with shapely body and a charming form.
But sometimes mightier courage dwells inside
a middling body, and illustrious power
transgresses all the body's limbs to rule
somewhere within obscure and darkened members.

[36] And so the queen, asked once for what she'd come,
whether she sought some great boon of the king,
responded that she'd come to fill her womb
and leave again to bear an offspring shared
with such a prince: she judged herself as worthy
that from her he might sire a kingdom's heirs.
If from that birth a noble woman issued,
the daughter would attain her mother's realms;
if there came forth a male, he'd be returned
for nourishment under his father's tutelage.

The king inquired whether Talestris cared
to take up arms beneath him, but she pleaded
her realm now lacked a guardian. Finally
she took the gift of thirteen nights, and gained
what she was seeking. Then she turned her steps
back to her realm's throne and ancestral cities.

[49] Bessus, meanwhile, had mobilized all Bactria.
Taking the crown, exchanging his old name,
he summoned Scythia and rose in arms.
The Macedonian seethed to hear such news;
and yet his ranks, sluggard with luxury,
weighed down with spoils of war, could scarce be moved.
He therefore judged a blaze must swallow everything
—a wondrous deed!—that might impede armed men.
He ordered first his own share to be carried
into his soldiers' midst. The field's broad plain
lay covered by that wealth brought forth in blood,
the labors of the Arabs and the Seres,
great wagons loaded with strange, various shapes.
Mars' hero seized a torch, and set the fire
upon the heaped wealth, mingling all with flames.
What they had saved so many times from burning,
opposing kindled cities' raging furnace,
so many times exerting all their strength
to endure the greedy blaze amidst much danger,
now burned by the consent of those same masters.
Yet rank and file dared not to mourn the cost
in bloodshed of those hard-won treasures, when
the king had burned his own wealth in the flames.
Once grief was laid to rest, it's said, they granted
that his command released the troops from care
and great unrest; the example of their lord
freed those with fire whom Lucre had enslaved.

[75] The disencumbered band now picked its route
toward Bactria, when, safe from foes without,
the unvanquished king came near to being slain
by his own consuls; yet he turned aside
his household's weapons and the civil outrage,
since Fate still spared him. Chief among his friends,

and greatest of the legion, stood Philotas,
seed of Parmenion, without whose aid
the king did nothing worthy of a song.
Three days he'd checked the rumor of the crime,
borne to him by report of Cebalinus,
until Metron revealed the outrage, and
Dimus' accomplices were bound, while he
himself fell on his sword. Philotas, too,
was cast in chains. By this sole circumstance
he was believed to seek the tyrant's murder:
that for two days he'd quashed the crime's report.
His hands bound at his back, his face concealed,
he now was led into the royal hall.
[90] The people, girt with arms, now came together
by royal edict, and the palace court
grew pale to see the fearsome steel. The ranks
all murmured, knowing nothing of such tumult,
nor why they had been summoned. With pricked ears
they waited, until Alexander broke
the silence to reveal the crime: he paused,
at first, when Dimus' corpse was carried in,
then said at last, "O citizens, I live
by Fortune's gift, though nearly had you lost me."
The hall broke into shouts at the king's words;
the crowds cried out, demanding he reveal
the authors of this crime. "Behold," he said,
"Parmenion, my father's special friend,
and mine as well, preferred by so much favor,
gave rise to this atrocity; Philotas,
conceiving such a hateful sacrilege
in concert with his father, chose as allies
Dimus, Demetrius, and Lecolaus,
and took the lead in hastening on my fate;
you see before you Dimus' wretched corpse."
Again the outraged assembly roared their fury.
Metron, Nicomachus, and Cebalinus
were brought as witnesses into their midst
to tell the crime's beginnings. "With what service,"
Mars' hero then continued, "has this man

esteemed his lord, with what zeal loved his father,
who kept his silence in foreknowledge of
this crime beyond all crimes? Yet Dimus' death
makes clear it should have been revealed. One hour
did not pass, after Cebalinus knew
the bitter outrage; yet Parmenion's son
alone gave it no credence, felt no fear:
clearly his father's power makes him haughty.
I set him over Media; now in pride
he hopes for greater things, aspiring to
the highest pinnacle of royal honor.
Bereft of kin, I have no freeborn offspring,
nor is my father living; this perchance
imbues Philotas' heart with fatal courage.
And yet, dire man, you err! While 'round me stand
so many ranks of Macedonia's generals,
do not suppose the Great One is bereaved.
Behold my brothers and my parents here!
His guilt is no less for the fact that Dimus
left out his name among the plot's participants.
This only proves they fear him as a leader
whom they might well betray. Though they confess
about themselves, of him they dare not speak,
hushed by their fear. Philotas has contrived
much doubtful talk of me, and lent his ears
to others of like words. He shares my joy,
he says, that Jupiter claims me as son,
but offers his condolences to those
who must live under princes of such arrogance,
who pass the goal and course of mortal rein.
I knew this, yet kept silent: for my part,
I did not wish those on whom I'd conferred
so many favors to become contemptible
in my eyes, or in others'. But rash speech
now turns to swords, and hand brings forth with steel
what then his mouth conceived. Where may I turn?
To whom shall I entrust my head? One man
I set above the many, and committed
my life and safety to him. Where I'd sought

protection, there I've found unlooked-for danger
to my own life. Far better, had I fallen
in battle, prey to enemies, than die
the victim of my fellow citizen.
Saved from those dangers that were all he feared,
the Macedonian falls among his comrades,
among the ranks whose arms he should not fear,
whose hands avoid. Therefore, my citizens,
I flee to your protection and your arms,
a citizen myself. May you become
the authors of my rescue. I cannot
find safety, nor would wish to do so, but
by your assent. If you desire to save me,
fulfill the avenger's duty and pass sentence."

[158] Such words of rage delivered, he abandoned
the council, ordering the bound Philotas
to be led forth in chains, lest any say
judicial process had lost all its force
in such a victor's court. So the man stood
with hands bound at his back, his color darkened,
his limbs concealed in tattered rags, his face
mournful—a man much changed from one who recently
had led the knights, second behind the king,
noblest among the splendid generals,
deployer of the ranks, and war's tactician.
In such guise, Flanders once saw Burchard pay
the rightful penalty of regicide:
the wheel of torture broke him for his crime,
twisting his limbs at Louis' vengeful bidding.
The ranks wavered in pity, overcome
with feeling for Parmenion's harsh fortune:
that noble man, deprived of his two offspring—
first Hector in his greatness, then Nicanor—
now ruled the Medes; the third son who remained,
his father's only balm, now pled his case
on barbarous shores before an unjust judge,
far from his sire. The princes' spirits wavered,
and savage sternness might have lost its force.
But then Amyntas, praetor of the king,

beheld their minds checked by their piety,
and so denounced Philotas, by his speech
reviving the flagged anger of the dukes,
stirring the rabble once again to savagery.

[185] And now stricken Philotas' powers failed:
he bent his gaze from the surrounding throng
and neither raised his head nor turned his eye,
perhaps because his guilty mind had lapsed,
perhaps because the fear of punishment
oppressed him. Fainting, he fell upon his guard.
At length, his mind restored, he took a cloth
to cleanse his tear-drenched face, and made reply:
"The guiltless easily find words, O citizens,
but checking misery's grief is no light task.
My mind, on one hand, rests within its port,
guiltless of all such crime, free of such knowledge;
upon the other, raging southern blasts
strike on my keel with surging waves. Between
these two, hedged in by either circumstance,
I see no way to satisfy at once
my innocence and what this hour requires.
If I obey harsh Fortune, I am done;
a stronger Fortune still forbids my mind
to stand forth guiltless: though itself secure,
my mind awaits the axe. Hope vies with fear,
and Fortune's shipwreck strives with safe deliverance.

[205] "What's more, I plead my case without my judge,
whom it would better serve to hear the merit
of innocence. I cannot see why he
absents himself, since only he can damn
the guilty man, or set the guiltless free.
I cannot be absolved, unless the judge
should sit to scrutinize the case; for scarcely
shall I be freed without him in whose presence
I first was bound. But though a man in chains,
who testifies before no magistrate,
has but a weak defense—he seems, indeed,
to accuse him of injustice—yet, as I'm able,
I'll plead on my behalf while death impends,

no traitor to myself. I cannot fathom
of what crime I am charged before this court.
None claims that I was numbered with the plotters
or their accomplices. Nicomachus
says nothing of me, still less Cebalinus,
who could have known no more, since he had learned
the outrage from the former. Still the king
denounces me as author of this crime.
Yet why would Dimus silently protect
the murderous plot's head, the master whom
he'd followed into such a dangerous juncture?
It scarcely has the ring of truth, that one
who does not spare himself should spare another.
More likely that, to save himself by recourse
to an illustrious name, Dimus might first
name me among the sharers of his guilt.
[229] "Old writings witness that when Ajax charged
the Ithacan with theft of Pallas' image,
Minerva's nighttime rape, he veiled his guilt
with Diomedes' name, excused the deed
because the son of Tydeus had lent aid.
Again, when Ajax claimed Laertes' son
had feigned insanity, and sought to hide
for fear of war, he answered, 'Let it shame me
that I have sought escape, if equal blame
is laid against Achilles, that he hid
among the women's ranks; I abnegate
no crime I share with such a mighty man.'
Thus, when the case of two is tried in common,
the greater sometimes exculpates the less.
[241] "You who are trained in jurisprudence, skilled
at law, declare what argument condemns
one whom no man accuses, by what statute
he merits death, against whom neither hearsay
nor his confession brings forth evidence.
Had Cebalinus not approached me first
with knowledge of this crime, I'd not be drawn
into the case today, though no one names me.
Yet it might be objected, 'You suppressed

a plot reported to you; to these rumors
you closed your ears.' What of it? Should I trust
the whinings of a boy? Words of great import
have lesser weight and value, when their author
wields no authority. Base origins
give such reports but trifling room for credence.
Had I shared Dimus' guilt, or known of it,
surely I would not have allowed myself
or the conspirators to be betrayed,
when for two days remained some chance of action.
I could have silenced Cebalinus secretly,
or in full view, lest he should bear the king
news of the undertaking. Though report
was brought to me of this endeavor, whose
disclosure could have meant my death, I entered,
alone, the king's apartments and his chamber,
bearing a sword. Why would I have postponed
the crime then? Or perhaps without Dimus
I dared not act? Philotas is believed
to shelter under him, and yet aspire
to seize the kingdom on the Great One's death!
But citizens, which of you has received
corruption's gift from me? Whom have I favored
more lavishly than any other of you?
    [268] "The king accuses me of writing to him
that I rejoiced in his great honor, whom
the voice of Jove claimed as his son; but offered
condolences to those whom Jupiter
placed under princes of such arrogance.
True loyalty and loyal love, freedom
of truthful counsel—deadly bane of some men—
benign reproof, the token of my love:
all these have deceived me. Philotas *did*
set down such things: I wrote them to the king,
not of him, sure that he more worthily
might own Jove with his silent vows, than rouse
the envy of great men against himself,
inciting princes' spleen with all his boasting.
    [280] "O king, what did it profit me to struggle

so many times upon the battlefield,
on your behalf, consuming all my youth
with you, and for you, in Mars' endless labor,
and losing my two brothers in the ranks?
I cannot claim my father in his absence,
appealing to him amidst all my troubles,
nor dare I plead his name, since he himself
is thought to share the guilt of the offense.
It's insufficient, clearly, that a father
should be deprived of his two sons, unless
he loses, too, the last who still remains,
and so is laid, guiltless, on his son's pyre.
Dear father, you will die on my account
and with me; I will bring about your death,
you who gave life to me. I'll break your thread,
a son extinguishing his father's age.
Why then did you create this lethal body?
Should you have not destroyed it, once created?
Could such fruit come but from an evil twig?
But who can say which lot deserves more pity,
a father's age, or his son's youth? Amidst
my spring's years, I am borne off from men's sight.
My father's spirit passes, his blood spent.
If Fortune had allowed a brief delay,
his wasted frame would render Nature's due."
He'd spoken thus, when lo! into the council
the king returned, surrounded by a host
clad in dark iron. Then in terror of
torment and death, his heart again was frozen,
and with a dead man's tongue he fell to earth.
[306] Doubt now began to creep among the princes,
and factions whispered wavering hesitation.
Some judged Parmenion's son should be destroyed
by stoning, as the ancient custom bade,
while others wished to find the truth by torture.
The latter's words were pleasing to the king,
who ordered the devices be prepared.
The torturers set their hands to every engine
of savagery, in full view of the wretch,

who blurted out, “O princes, there’s no need
of a severer scourge. Here I confess it—
I wished it done.” But when still graver torments
assailed him, when no place upon his body
was left to feel a wound, and naked bones
thrust through the tattered flesh to take the blows,
at last he told the details of the plot,
its master plan and goal. Yet it was doubtful
whether he had confessed such monstrous crimes
to spare himself excruciating hours,
and end his pains with death’s swifter approach.
[323] With what laborious strife does fluid chance
advance the deeds of mortals! With what ease
it casts down those whom it has let ascend!
With mighty effort, Fortune raised Philotas
up from the nation’s midst; Parmenion’s seed
became commander, leading all the host,
yet after a short season fell. An exile
condemned by Fate, rocks crushed him, even as
he strove to rise. All hands together vied
to cast their stones against him, from whose hand
had previously come the encampment’s marching orders.
How meaningless the glory of all things,
how fleeting worldly honor’s empty titles!
In power lies no will to do men good.
[335] After Philotas’ death, six days had passed,
when Alexander hastened in pursuit
of Bessus, sparing nothing to fulfill
the office of Fate’s universal hammer.
Unceasingly he plied his rapid course,
until that raging monster had been flushed
from eastern lairs, and set in chains before him.
The frenzied Macedonian then beheld him
completely stripped, his neck and feet in irons:
“What bestial madness, Bessus, or what Fury
urged you to such a crime, that you dared bind
a king so worthy, coveting his realm,
and with the sword of violence closed the life
of your own lord and father?” So he spoke,

and summoned Darius' brother, whom earth's conqueror
had long employed among his bodyguards.
Receiving Bessus bound in hand and foot,
the man drew forth his cursed soul with long tortures,
and soothed his brother's shade with blood, invoking
the Stygian sisters for the rites. So Bessus
was sent to Tartarus upon a cross.
Such was his death: while Bessus strove to rise,
he fell into the depths, returning to
his proper station even while he ruled,
a slave affecting the insignia of his lord.

[358] Still Alexander thirsted in his heart
for Scythia's realm, and swifter than a leopard
advanced his columns to the Tanais,
whose eddying vastness separates that kingdom
from Bactria, and by its sundering waves
divides all Europe from the Asian lands.
Its people are Sarmatians. If reports
from long ago are worthy of some trust,
they live on mountains, using for their chambers
and halls the fearsome lairs of savage beasts,
contemptuous of gain, content with food
such as Nature herself bestows, refusing
to sully with ambition's curse the blessings
of such a life. While still the Macedonian
was laying out his camp, in preparation
to breach the width of Tanais, the channel
that he would cross the next day into battle
upon the Scythian shore, lo! twenty men
came bearing to the king their charge, all clothed
in foreign garb, and riding shaggy mounts.

[374] The oldest of them gazed upon the king
and thus addressed him: "If your body suited
your soul and mind, which grasp after enormities,
if your tremendous frame matched what you covet,
the whole vast world could never give you space;
your stature would exceed all earthly bounds,
your right hand seize the East, your left the West.

Scarcely content with that, your heart would burn
to seek out and observe the sun's far hiding.
You'd dare to mount that light's miraculous car,
guiding the stars in downcast Phoebus' stead.
Thus, thus, you long for much you do not grasp.
The earth subdued, the human race enslaved,
with gory arms you'll move against the trees,
against the stones and beasts. You'll not permit
the snowy mountains or the monsters, lurking
amidst their crags, to go unscathed, but even
the insensate elements will feel your fury.
Or don't you know, the strength of a great tree
can be thrown over in a single hour,
though long it's challenged heaven, haughty in
its mighty roots, though vast of branch it grows?
Only the fool refuses to assess
the tree's height, as he gazes at the fruit.
Take care, that while you aim to reach its crown,
you do not fall amidst its shattered branches,
once you've attained it. Often will the lion
become a banquet for the little birds,
though once the lord of beasts; and iron,
though harder still than bronze or any metal,
is yet consumed by rust. Thus, under Phoebus
nothing's so strong that ruin does not threaten
from something that is weaker of itself.
Who sails the world, yet has no need to fear
the storm, or death's approach? What has our life
to do with you? We have not taken arms,
or set foot in your land to do you battle.
The Scythians, who shun arms and the din
of human concourse, dwelling in their caves
and shady groves, know not (so be it always!)
who you may be, or whence you had your birth,
whence you have come, or to what end you're sent.

[409] "Our land's free race desires nothing more
than what Nature, our first source, has bestowed.
In virtue of her gift, we neither serve

nor seek to rule. Such practice brings us blessing:
that each man is a law unto himself,
protecting his own folk and goods, content
with their possession, wanting no one else's.
If more than this you seek, your will exceeds
the boundaries of true beatitude.
[416] "But know the customs of the Scythian race:
cattle we have, and plows, bowls, spears, and arrows.
Amongst both friends and foes we use these things.
From goblets we drink wine in honor of
the holy gods; with friends we share our grain,
brought forth by labor of our cattle. From
a distance we destroy our enemies
with arrows; closer up, we use the spear.
[422] "What land can hold you? Which, pray, will suffice?
You've conquered Lydia and Cappadocia,
vanquished the Persians, Medes, and Syrians,
along with Bactria, and now, victorious,
you pass toward India. For shame, that you
reach out your greedy and inconstant hands
for our cattle. All realms deal out their wealth
to you, yet to yourself you seem a pauper.
What need have you of riches, which engender
in greedy men yet greater hunger? Thus
the more you have accrued, the fiercer burns
your love of having; thus you sate your appetite,
and plenty fosters want. Do you forget
how long the Bactrians have checked your course?
While you subdue one people, others rise.
Victory's born of war, yet in her turn
she brings you war again. To find new foes
and conquer Scythia, a land long free,
you'll cross the Tanais. And yet our poverty
is swifter than your troops. The wealth and booty
of all the world is laden on your army;
we carry little and more swiftly flee,
more swiftly put to flight. When you imagine
that we are far away, within your camp
you'll find the Scythians; when you suppose

the foe's been captured, or can easily
be taken, swifter than the Eastern wind
they'll flee your grasp. No greed, no opulence
allures the Scythians, a race of men
who scorn cities and towns, and nothing know
of human concourse, dwelling in the wastes.
[448] "Remember, then, to grasp your Fortune closely,
grip tight her hand: she's thin and slippery,
and never can be held unwillingly.
Pursue the healthful counsel of the moment:
while still your hand can throw a lucky cast,
before you've cause to chide swift-moving Fortune,
impose a limit on your conquering arms,
lest soon the wheel should overturn your labors.
Among us, Fortune's said to have no feet:
we draw her having feathered hands and arms.
So if she stretches out her hand to you,
hold fast her wings, lest she should fly away
whenever she desires. If you be god,
your nature should require benevolence
toward mortals, and you should bestow your bounty,
not take away what's theirs. But if you're human,
and so like us, you should always recall
that which you truly are. What foolishness,
to give your mind to what makes you forgetful
of your own self! You'll have as friends all those
on whom you wage no war. The bonds of love
remain firmest between peers. They are equals
who do not yield, nor yet outstrip each other,
who spawn for one another by their strength
no perils of blood-spattered Mars. Beware
lest you imagine you can count as friends
those you have vanquished. Sooner shall the earth
contain the stars, sooner the Ocean drown
the Dipper's seven lights, sooner shall fish
crawl on dry land, than slaves enjoy a bond
of true love with their masters. Concord never
shall stand between them. Though in outward show
peace may prevail, hatred surges within.

Beneath such guise of peace, hearts foment war."
[477] Thus he spoke, but still the Macedonian
deployed his columns, and prepared to turn
his arms against the Scythians. Crossing over
the river in full force, he met the foe
and—not without the bloodshed of his men—
at length compelled all Scythia to serve
the Macedonian sway. Just so, among
the Alpine rocks, a fir of aged strength
grows toward the stars: unbent for many years,
despising blasts from east and west and south,
it's taxed perchance by Boreas' chill breath,
which whips the air according to its wont;
its ancient limbs and moss-encrusted trunk
avail it nothing—uprooted, it strikes
the earth with prostrate crown. So, too, although
the Scythians had broken the assaults
of Medes, of Persia and Assyria,
yet they succumbed to Alexander, when
that bloody sword of fate, the world's lone scourge,
fell on them swifter and more savagely
than Boreas' icy wings. So fate decreed.
[496] Among the neighboring tribes, swift Rumor prattled
the news of such a triumph, and at once
their hearts imbibed new fear, while all the world
stood terrified. Among the lands that lay
under the rising Phoebus, many passed
of their own will beneath the Grecian yoke,
since they had heard of Scythia's defeat,
that land before unbroken by harsh war,
but now subjected to the Macedonians.
They thought no other princes of like might,
or equal strength of soul, remained on earth,
now that they'd seen unmastered Scythia's fall.
Yet men's submission to his yoke was due
no more to arms, than to his mercy toward
the vanquished; for in truth, the Great One bound
by force of love all those that he had conquered.

Without harshness, without demanding greed,
moved by their pleas, he freely sent home captives
and pardoned criminals, to show thereby
that he had joined a savage race in combat
to test his mettle, not to slake his wrath.

Book Nine

The Headings of the Ninth Book

The Great One in the ninth book masses strength
and marches against India, but Porus
staves off by mighty arms gods' will and Fate.
Two youths in death plunge either host in mourning.
When Alexander's gained the hostile shore,
the armies clash. At last, Porus is broken,
and with him all the tyrants of the Orient.
The Great One's marvelous leap brings Greek sedition;
more marvelous still, that wondrous mind's proposal
dispatches cohorts to new feats of arms.

Book Nine

The last to feel the Macedonian onslaught,
still India remained to be subdued
by dint of labor and by savage war.
But while that rival of the gods on earth
still sought her, Clitus, Hermolaus, and
that teacher second only to great Aristotle
beheld their final day, a clear lesson
to coming generations: for indeed,
their end attests the transient faith of kings.
[9] Nearly the whole of India lies under
the newborn sun. She gazes, head held high,
upon the reaches of the East; but where

she looks down upon Libya and the south,
the earth rises towards high heaven's vault.
Elsewhere, the plains lie low: here Caucasus
of mighty fame sends forth its rushing streams,
and, colder than the rest, the Indus flows,
from which the land acquired its name. The Ganges
pours down in headlong torrents from the ridge
of mountains in the south, greatest of rivers
in all the East. Both surge tumultuously
into the Red Sea, ripping up great oaks,
and swallowing the soil that holds their roots.
Soft earth encountered by their puissant waves
retards their course; the island that is formed
absorbs the flow. The Ganges intercepts
the Achesis as it flows down to the sea.
They meet with huge commotion, and between them
the current seethes; and if one should believe
swift Rumor, there the waters wash up gold
and gems—such substances as in our day
command a dearer price than is their due.
Thence comes the opulence of eastern tribes;
for when loquacious Fame noised it abroad
that with such goods the Indies were endowed,
all nations of the earth ran forward swiftly
to buy those smiling gems, offscourings of
the ruddy strait, themselves of little worth,
which human greed alone has rendered precious.
So then the Indian dukes heard with amazement
that Jove's Pellaean son had landed there,
the scourge of every kingdom in the world.
They gathered, plunged in fear, to calm that god
with offerings of cities crammed with wealth.
Among them on those shores, only Porus
made ready to oppose him strenuously,
just as a shattered Alpine mountain peak
falls down the heights, and on its twisting course
breaks rocks athwart its path; but if a mass
of stone whose roots pierce to some Stygian recess,

itself a mountain, lies across its way,
they shudder hideously, and crash like thunder.
[48] So Alexander heard that with armed might
Porus stood watch upon the Indian marches,
and kept the guise of war with all his strength.
On headlong course he then sought out the swift
Hydaspes, filled with joy that Porus stood
upon the farther bank in gathered force,
where serried ranks proffered the stuff of triumph.
A fearsome elephant of untold mass,
still vaster and more horrid than the others,
conveyed the king, whose golden arms, inlaid
with snow-white metal, shielded one whose body
surpassed the limits of the human frame.
His spirit was the equal of his limbs,
and as in height, so by his prudence, he
exceeded India's peers. The Grecian ranks
felt terror both of that fierce host, and of
the crossing of the river's surging depths.
It bore the likeness of the thundering sea:
an image of the deep, the wide Hydaspes
lay half a mile in breadth, unfordable
and deep of channel. Only boats could cross it,
but opposite the barbarous host was waiting
to rain its weapons like a lethal cloud
into their midst, and so with ease avert
the ships from landing on the bank they sought.
[71] Amidst the river, rooted in the earth,
there lay a large island. From either army
the young swam out, their limbs weighed down by arms,
to test their prowess in a minor skirmish.
Thus with a risk of negligible import
they prefaced the great onslaught yet to come.
[77] Within the Macedonian encampment—
a matter worthy to relate—two men
alike in body as in soul, Nicanor
and Symachus, were thought to have been born
upon a single day. Love bound them both

with equal force, as did the work of war,
and equally in every gain or loss
they took their chance in strife. With close-joined shields
they went forth, whether ordered to build up
bulwarks against the enemy, to launch
stones from the catapult, or break down walls.
Sent out to gather stores, or to besiege
the enemy with trenches, to deceive
the foe by night, to take the watch, or scout
the ambush hidden in a gorge, they met
whatever dangers war had offered them,
all its uncertain efforts, as a pair
of comrades linked in body and in soul.
So, goaded on by youth, these men's green spirits
prepared at length to prattle of some plan
conceived in their great heart, and Symachus
spoke first, and keenly: "Do you see, Nicanor,
how at a scanty river's barrier
the glory sticks of our unvanquished king?
Some daring deed's required to crown our brow
with victor's laurel, if by our own strength
we drive the enemy from river's edge;
or else to clothe us, though stripped of our bodies,
in endless fame, should Fate hold such in store."
Nicanor broke in when he'd scarcely spoken:
"The gods witness that with a silent mind
I too have long intended such deeds. Now
with no delay let's rush upon the foe,
content with light equipment." Saying no more,
girded with swords, they braved the rushing currents.
Their lances bobbed behind them, and under
their leadership a large band swam the river.
When they had reached the nearby isle, the sky
echoed with mingled shouts, where hostile forces
had laid a prior claim in no small numbers.
They met the Indians, and like a hailstorm
spears flew, and bore death through the empty air.
But Symachus, the first to swim across,
attacked the foe with drawn sword, while Nicanor

strove to bedeck the earth with many a corpse.
Now blades had done enough, now spears were ruddy,
the river's current was streaked purple; but
within no bounds is rash strength satisfied.

[118] They still exulted over conquered foes,
when, stealthily, more Indians crept forward
to aid their dying fellows. This was grief
and mournful ruin for the Grecian ranks.
Andromachus was slain, scion of kings;
three times five knights of splendid title fell,
for whose death all Greece wept with drawn-out tears.
Those two of Grecian birth alone remained,
brothers if not in blood, then in their spirit,
partners in life and in approaching death.
While round them pressed a shower of javelins,
their minds, amazed, stuck on a course of action.
The two held neither spear nor lance, which lay
broken in fragments. Only their swords remained,
and these they wielded, precipitously rushing
against the foe. But darts imbedded in
their youthful limbs held back their steps, preventing
them from dispatching Mars' work in close combat.
Since they beheld their final doom's approach,
each man now prayed he might be first to die,
falling before his friend: to see his death
seemed crueler to him than oblivion.
Each cast himself before the other, striving
to slow his comrade's end. While each leapt forward,
while this one shielded that, and that one this,
lo! through the air, hurled by a giant's arm,
a shaft of fir-wood flew amidst their strivings,
pinning them both to earth. Thus undivided,
their youth lay plaited by a spear, nor did
their endless love recede even in death.
They passed amidst their kisses and embrace,
each dying doubly in his friend's demise.
At last, relinquishing their limbs, they trod
the narrow path towards Elysian fields.

[148] The victory of his men raised Porus' breast

in its indomitable zeal, nor yet
drove Alexander, that downfall of kings,
despiser of all peril, to despair.
With silent heart, he weighed a stratagem
by which he might cross over to meet Porus.
Among so many thousands, one man, Attalus,
seemed closest to the king in face and body,
and Alexander ordered him be garbed
in royal finery, that he might stand
upon the bank, and offer the appearance
to Porus, as he looked on, that the king
remained there, and no longer was concerned
to find a means of crossing. But the king
passed far beyond that stretch of river, leaving
the Macedonian encampment: thus
he might deceive the enemy, content
with few companions. And the powers on high
abetted the great Duke's intention—wrapping
the elements in blind shadow, a cloud
spread out across the world. Such darkness covered
the troops beneath it, that no man could know
another's face as he addressed him. Others
might find in such a cloud the source of terror,
seeing that, over unknown waters, boats
must be conveyed; but while that darkened air
might frighten such men, in full confidence
the Macedonian ordered the first craft,
in which he rode, be launched with oars upraised
into the current. With no more delay,
the crowd of soldiers thronged around the duke
upon the river: landing on the bank
where no foe stood, they took up arms and, armed,
rushed forth upon the foe. But Porus still
looked to the other bank, where earlier
he'd fixed his gaze on Attalus, who'd shone
in royal raiment. Now a messenger
brought word to him: the Macedonian king
approached, and with him, too, the final outcome.

[179] When dawn broke clearer through the thickened clouds,

and the opposing phalanx flashed forth brightly
in Phoebus' light, Porus beheld the foe,
and sent against them twice two thousand knights;
sent, too, a hundred war-cars full of men
longing for blood, who scattered far and wide
whole clouds of javelins, which rained down death
and lamentation. But because the storm's
still recent force had left the ground too soft,
the chariots with their heavy burden stuck
in muddy ground, and were of little use.
But on the other side, the Macedonian
pressed through the Indian ranks with wonted speed.
His light battalion and his vanguard band
pursued him in his rush. Commingled shouts
and trumpets' clangor rose, but from the Greeks
came back the sound of beating drums. The ranks
on either side fell down in writhing death.
Two of the fateful sisters scarce sufficed
to spin the threads the third so quickly broke.
    [196] Yulcon, son of Enax, was the first
to loose his reins and challenge Alexander,
taxing his breathless elephant with goads.
He died pierced by a spear, while tirelessly
Mars' hero picked a course toward Porus, through
so many intervening foes. He spied him
astride an elephant, like some great citadel
preeminent above defending walls,
and said, still at a distance, "Here, at last,
is danger worthy of amazement, and
my spirit's match. One deed I must achieve
against both monsters and illustrious men."
    [206] He spoke, and toward the left flank turned his track:
there warlike tumult vexed the air more gravely,
where Porus battled; fighting men pursued him,
Ariston and Polidamas, his fellow.
Stricken by Ariston's sword blow, Rubricus
now rubricated earth with his own blood.
Candaceus took up a giant pike,
intending to destroy Polidamas;

but intercepted by the shaft of Glaucus,
he murmured, dying, to the soggy earth.
And now the Argive phalanx broke its way
into the Indian ranks, whose lines scarce held,
their first force spent. But towering elephants
were loosed at Porus' order on the cavalry,
though such a sluggish animal, one nearly
incapable of movement, could not equal
the horses' flying gait. The Greeks came 'round
to strike the foe and, with a loosened rein
avoided the attack. Nor could the savages
employ arrows in combat, for their bow,
a huge and heavy thing, must needs be pressed
into the earth: unless flexed from beneath,
no man could bend it. Now the Indians
scorned Porus' lordship (as is known to happen
when ranks are routed: dread commands more fiercely
than any duke). Some bade the troops fan out,
while others said hold firm, or close the ranks.
Among so many thousands, none commanded.
Yet Porus gathered once again his forces,
deployed his ranks, and cast the elephants,
a fearsome sight, against the enemy.
The monsters brought the Greeks no little terror:
their horrid shrieking moved both beasts and men;
the air itself grew terrified and trembled.
Now strident sounds of terror shook the troops
as ranks were broken; now they made to flee
who recently had held the upper hand,
but Alexander mustered the slack columns,
bidding the Agrian and Thracian knights
to turn upon the monsters in attack.
At once courage revived; laying aside
the fear of death, their prowess swelled in combat
against great odds. The hand emptied the quiver,
and fatal arrows flew with bloody death
against both men and monsters. Eagerly,
but with too little caution, some men followed:
trampled by elephants, they left sure witness

their fellows should advance more cautiously.
[248] With no small loss of Macedonian blood,
the headlong battle raged, until as one
they all began to wield axes against
the elephants' firm feet, and with curved blades
hack at their hideous trunks. At length, exhausted
by darts, and overcome with bloody wounds,
both mounts and riders fell in one swift crash.
Then mindlessly the host took flight in terror,
deserting Porus, while he yet rained down
thick clouds of missiles from atop his monster,
like one alone upon the open sea.
And when he was assailed from every side,
gashed everywhere, and bleeding from nine wounds
that gaped wide open in his several limbs,
his driver saw the tyrant weakening.
He goaded on the elephant to flight,
while Alexander, like God's lightning wrath,
bore down upon the fugitive. But Bucephal
died in the midst of that pursuit, pierced through
by bloody showers of weapons; as he fell,
he set the king upon his feet, despite
his failing legs: he was the only mount
worthy of such a prince, and not long after,
Pellaeus named a city in his honor.
[269] More slowly then, upon another horse
the king moved after Porus and his men.
Now Taxiles, who ruled the Indians,
a king himself, but well disposed toward him
whom Fortune had disposed to rule the world,
had there a brother, who bade Porus yield
to Fortune, and surrender to a foe
both so illustrious and so mild of will.
Porus, though weakened by the loss of blood,
by happy circumstance was yet aroused
to answer the familiar voice, and said,
"Are you—for shame!—the brother of Taxiles,
who like some fugitive betrayed my person
and his own sovereignty?" He spoke, and cast

against his foe the only weapon that
had not yet fallen from his hands. It took
the youth full in the breast, burst through his back,
and lulled his eyes into eternal sleep.
[283] Again he took to flight; but overcome
by many wounds, his beast gave out entirely,
and cast him down on foot before the foe,
the Great One who pursued him. Alexander
supposed him dead, and bade the noble corpse
be plundered. But the elephant began
to assail the spoilers with its savage tusks,
and set the half-dead man upon its back,
until its guts, now bristling with javelins,
poured out its life. The king, who'd thought that Porus
now wandered with the peoples of Avernus,
beheld him raise his eyes with steady gaze.
He vanquished hate with kindness, and spoke thus:
"Porus, what drunken mindlessness perverts
your senses, that in such great pride you dared
oppose me with your banners raised, although
you knew the reputation of my deeds?"
But Porus answered, "Great One, since you ask,
and in your asking grant such liberty
as I can claim—before this struggle's ills
I thought no man on earth could check my power,
nor equal me in battle or in thought.
I knew my strength and worth, but had not yet
made trial of your fate and strength. Then war
taught by its outcome you were stronger still—
and yet I count myself blessed not a little,
as one subordinate to you alone.
But such a circumstance—that you have won—
should not raise up your spirit. Let me serve
as an example to you—I, who found
one stronger than my own most mighty self.
Do not call that one blessed who waxes great,
unless he has it not in him to wane.
Better not to ascend, than to retreat

after the ascent; better not to swell
than to diminish after that increase.
The greedy are more gravely tortured, knowing
what they have lost, than having gave them pleasure.
Rein in your course, then. Fortune's benefits
shall fail—unsure the knowledge of her favor."
[317] The Macedonian wondered that the king
remained unbroken amidst Fortune's tumult,
showing, though conquered, an unvanquished spirit.
Therefore he curbed his wrath, his heart transformed.
Against all expectations of the nobles,
he generously healed the sick man's wounds,
supported him in convalescence, and
received him courteously, when he was strong,
among the assembled number of his friends.
More liberally still, he made yet wider
the limits of his sway: his foe received
such honor as a friend might scarce expect.
[326] When Porus had submitted to that conquest,
though great of heart and previously unvanquished,
the Macedonian swelled in pride: upon him
had Fortune lavished such a famous triumph,
that he supposed all countries of the East
now lay open before him. On he rushed
with slackened rein, to turn his martial prowess
against the farthest races of the world,
and join vast Ocean's peoples to his empire.
So swifter than the East Wind, he descended
upon the Indies and the world's far climes,
traversing various peoples with their kings.
To human minds he seemed no less a portent,
nor brought less terror, than nocturnal lightning,
whose flash is followed by the din and clash
of shattered cloud, when far-flung thunder moves
the pallid world, and terrifies the wretch
who lies in woe, remembering some guilt.
[341] Yet still the race of the Sudracae dared
oppose fate and the Greeks' fierce reputation;

they feared to risk a doubtful battle's outcome,
and shut themselves in their strong city's walls.
While others hesitated, Alexander
moved up the ladders he had ordered set
against the hostile rampart. But the space
was narrow, and the wall scarcely afforded
a place to stand: he clung upon the height.
A thousand darts, hurled from the turrets, pressed him,
while none among the Macedonian host
could climb the rungs as that fierce shower fell.
At length, shame and the rout of the first ranks
conquered the danger and the force of weapons.
The tardy succour of his lagging troops
compelled him to face either foe or death.
In droves they struggled to climb up, forgetting
their love of life; but by their haste assistance
was further still delayed—for while they strove
to mount the steps, the ladders were weighed down:
they shattered, and the whole cohort collapsed
one on another. The sight of Alexander
standing alone, as though amidst a wasteland,
turned Macedonian hopes into despair.
His hand, which held the shield to ward off blows,
threatened to fail, exhausted, and his comrades
shouted that he should quickly leap into
their waiting arms. But now the king dared something
wondrous to tell (too great, perhaps, for credence):
he plunged into that city filled with savages
headlong in one fell leap, deeming it shameful
a prince descended from the gods, possessed
of such great titles, should not face the enemy.
One might well ask whether the king was proven
courageous or foolhardy by that deed;
if you prefer to join contrary terms,
then he was both courageous and foolhardy,
and though before he rose they might have killed him,
or taken him alive, amazing Fortune
defended him from either fate, and shielded
her foster son in wonderful degree.

[377] For Alexander, balancing himself,
landed upon his feet, and stood in challenge.
Almighty Fortune had provided that
the foe could not attack him from behind:
as though it had grown up to shield the duke
among its aged limbs, thick-set of branch,
a laurel stood there. The unconquerable hero
kept to its trunk, while heaven's retribution
swung 'round the shield, and warded off the blows
of flying weapons. Though from far away
they all attacked him, none dared to approach
more closely, or to strike with his own hand.
The wide-spread fear of his illustrious name,
which now had sounded through the conquered world,
fought on the duke's behalf—and desperation,
that goad to valor, and the opportunity
for death with honor. But a rain of darts
had now gouged through the shield; his helmet groaned
with blows from storms of rocks. His knees gave way
and in the burden of that constant labor
could scarcely bear his noble body's weight.
When those who stood nearby prepared to strip him,
the Great One so received them with his sword
that two lay dead before him. At their death
the Sudracae stood aghast, so that none dared
attack the great man with their gathered strength.
Still like a tiger, with no feeble force,
though sunk upon his knees, he turned aside
all the blows his body might have suffered,
until an arrow, flagrant in its crime,
sped through the void, and stuck in his right side.
The king, maddened and trembling, could not draw
the arrow with his wavering right hand,
so much blood poured out from the wound's raw mouth.
Near death, he laid his bloodless joints against
the laurel, and cast down his arms. The Indian
who'd shot the dart supposed the king now dead;
he ran delighted to despoil the corpse.
But when the Macedonian sensed that hand

approaching toward him with profane intent,
he spoke again: "Do you not recognize
the Macedonian duke?" With no more words
he summoned back his failing spirit, and
slashed through his foe's bare flank with thrusting sword point,
uniting him in death with his two fellows.
"That such a one should pass among the shades
is fitting," Alexander said. "Let such
a man serve as my messenger." He'd spoken,
and that he might fight on unconquered, till
his sacred spirit fled in the thin air,
he strove to raise himself upon his shield,
and on the laurel's boughs. Yet even thus,
he could not lift his noble weight, but fell
again on sinking knees, taunting the foe
if any dared do battle with drawn iron,
and claim the spoil of such a victory.
[426] At last Peucestes, following the wall,
attacked the town's defenders further on.
He burst with vigor through the passages,
and reached the inner courts with sword unsheathed.
When Alexander's failing eye beheld him,
he saw no hope for life, but thought a comrade
in death had reached him. On his tottering shield
he raised his body; then Timaeus came,
and finally Leonnatus and Ariston.
They burned to guard the king with all their strength
against the gathered Indians. But while
all on their own, they pressed back many thousands,
Timaeus fell, illustrious in war;
Peucestes took a grave wound to his head,
and Leonnatus fell. Their arms cast down,
they lay before the king's feet, and Ariston
remained the only hope, but even he
was wounded as the Indians surged on:
he scarcely could hold back such savage fury.
[442] Swift Rumor, meanwhile, brought news to the Greeks:
their duke had fallen within the fortress walls.
They were aroused by such a dire report,

which might have broken other men with fear.
Forgetting every danger, they broke through
the wall with picks and made an entrance, scorning
the threat of death. Their road lay through the wall.
On all sides, crowds were slaughtered. No distinction
was made of age or sex. All whom they met
they deemed the source of Alexander's wound,
or of his death. The tireless sword raged on,
until no foe remained in all the wrack,
or stood exposed to the avenging hand.
[453] Without delay, the eager princes ran
to bring assistance to the prone Pellaean.
They carried back that envy of the gods
into the camp. Critobolus, one great
among physicians, bared the wound. He found
a hooked blade buried in the flesh; unless
by skill of hand, he cut a greater wound,
he could not extricate it. So he trembled,
imagining the flow of blood that might
surge forth as he withdrew the tip. Dumbstruck,
he saw his fate loom up before him, should
he treat the king ineptly, all the ills
that threatened now to fall upon his head.
The king regarded his astonishment,
his wavering mind, the tears dried with his cloak:
"If such a wound cannot be healed, why hesitate
at least to free me of a lingering death?
Or do you fear the consequences, if
you bring to me a swift though mortal succor?"
The other man—whether he feared no longer,
or kept his terror to himself—now begged
the king to let himself be steadied, till
he'd drawn the barbs out, for the slightest movement
might bring no little danger to his life.
"Critobolus, unseemly is it ever
to bind or hold a king," the other answered.
"His power must remain both free and sound."
[477] He'd spoken, and—you'd scarcely dare believe this—
he held himself unmoving, while his face

betrayed no crease in token of the pain.
But when the point was drawn out, copious blood
gushed from the opened wound, and darkness closed
upon his eyes. His wavering spirit hovered
in such an agony that round about him
his friends could scarcely hear his failing whisper.
A mournful tumult spread throughout the camp,
soon as the news was heard. The Grecian youths
fell down in lamentation, crying out
that his one life was life to all. The clamor
grew silent only when Critobolus
employed his skill to staunch the flow with herbs.
At last, then, could the Great One fall to slumber;
at last, then, when the camp had heard report
the king was safe, his men banished their sadness,
and laid out tables for a lavish feast
through all their companies. Just so, a clamor
goes up upon the deep Aegean, when
the sky, it seems, would pour down stinking pitch;
the North Wind revels, and the helmsman tumbles
head first over the broken stern into
the surging waves; they shout, and each man fears
a common ruin, declaring that all die
in one man's death. But if their grappling hooks
drag that man back alive, and they repair
the rudder, joyous tumult fills the air,
and new rejoicing cancels earlier grief.
[501] Few days had passed after the treatment of
Pellaeus' wound. Still might some graver illness
arise before the scab had thickened over,
and yet, impatient of delay, he readied
swift arms against the races of the Ocean:
once he'd subdued the birthplace of the sun,
he'd seek the Nile's source, unknown to mortals.
The task of making ready a great fleet
fell to the Indian kings, Abissares
and Porus, with the help of Taxiles.
Report of it filled the astonished ears

of all the army. When the generals
took counsel for their welfare and the king's,
the exhausted dukes advanced as in a column,
and now Craterus carried their entreaties
before him. "Mighty king, for whom this world,
though vast, can never suffice—what limit will
your power and the hunger of your mind
set for themselves, what boundary will they honor?
If you scorn your own safety—and you do—
if it has lost its value, at the least,
O Great One, let the welfare of your men
be precious to you. Let all races plot
our slaughter; let the fleets obscure the deep,
let beasts sharpen their poisoned fangs, let monsters
attack in strange, uncanny forms; expose
us to all perils of the land and sea,
but save yourself alone, take pains to spare
your own life. Who can lead us, as we pass
continuously, so many times unconquered,
into new dangers? Favorable circumstance
permits no man to stand forever still.
What god would dare to promise that you'll be
the Macedonians' abiding star?
Who could long keep you safe, as on you plunge
amidst the world's mishaps? Why do you rush
upon such risks to seize some squalid village?
When labor and reward are balanced equally,
and gains are matched in like amounts by loss,
the goods one holds are sweeter in prosperity,
and in adversity a greater solace.
Henceforth, in your own person be more sparing
of both yourself and us. Expose us to
whatever prodigy you will; avoid
a sordid war, mean battles, and bleak peril.
Ignoble foes will tarnish any glory.
Unworthy is it that your strength or glory
should be consumed, brought forth, as it has been,
in greatest labor, amidst such undertakings

as shun men's sight." So also Ptolemy
and all the council pleaded, choked with tears.
[545] The devotion of his men was not unwelcome,
and so he spoke: "No little debt I owe,
nor shall I be ungrateful to you, generals—
first, since I know today you have preferred
my safety to your own, but even more
because you've spared no token of your faith
or love toward me, from my reign's first inception,
or from the war's beginning. But my mind
and yours are not the same, nor do I wish
to leave off what's begun, or to conclude
the war. A lifespan won't contain me; neither
by length of life nor by this age's laws,
do I take measure of myself. My glory
exceeds this age's limits; glory alone
I choose to be the measure of your king.
Unworthy spirits and ignoble breasts
believe the highest good lies in long life.
But I, the world's one king, who count my triumphs,
and not my years, in thousands, have already
enjoyed a long life, if I contemplate
my famous deeds. I've conquered Thrace and Asia.
The boundary of the world lies near at hand.
Not to provoke the ill will of the gods,
the world's too narrow, and the breadth of earth
is insufficient for its only lord.
But when I've passed beyond this conquered universe,
I'll undertake to open to my followers
another world. The strong man finds no goal
insuperable. I hasten now to penetrate
the shores of the Antipodes, and view
the other Nature. Though you begrudge your arms,
I cannot fail in duty to myself.
I'll think the entire world my theater,
and move my troops throughout its length, ennobling
ignoble lands and peoples by my wars.
While I stand as your duke, your feet will trample
lands hidden from all races by great Nature.

It is my will to face these tasks—yes, even
if Fortune see fit in these undertakings
to end a fleeting but illustrious life."
He'd spoken, and now summoned his companions
to board the ship; they urged that he should lead them
wherever he desired. And lo! the clamor
of sailors rose up from the estuary.

Book Ten

The Headings of the Tenth Book

The tenth book vexes Ocean with bold fleets.
Infernal Chaos and Gehenna's citizens
are moved by Nature's plaint and warnings. When
the Ocean's tamed, the Great One's breast considers
stupendous feats, and readies a flotilla
to break the Western World in battle. Terrified,
the earth assembles and dispatches tribute.
By poison's agency the Great One's conquered,
whom sword had not subdued. Freed from its bonds
of clay, his spirit flies to heaven's air.

Book Ten

Now Zephyr sent the ships a star-filled swell
and favorable current. Out of port
the straining sailor pushed the fleet still farther,
unknowing where the course led, or how far
yet lay the flow of Ocean's untried stream.
That same while, Nature with a mindful grief
recalled how both the world and she herself
had suffered insult from the prince, who'd called
the earth too narrow and prepared armed throngs
to lay open her secret parts. Distressed,
her noble white hair tangled, she left off
her latest works, the figures she'd begun

to form of Matter, and in rage she ceased
instilling souls into diverse limbs. Veiled
in cloudy mantle, toward the Styx she turned,
and to the hidden kingdoms of the second world.
The elements gave quarter where she trod
and rose to meet their Shaper. Newly calmed,
the air worshipped the advent of the goddess.
In vernal pleasure Earth's flowers burst forth,
the sea reined in the waves more than its wont,
and now the tumid billows held their silence.
All things bestowed on Nature worthy honor,
praying that what she'd sown she'd multiply,
and grant increase unto the seeds of things,
infusing warmth and moisture. Paying thanks
to her creatures, she bade them keep her laws
and in nothing exceed the bounds she'd set.
"To Styx I shall descend to save my own,"
she said, "and seek the head of Alexander,
our common scourge, whom sea and land abhor."
She opened then dark fissures in the earth,
and on the sloping path sought Tartarus.
[31] Before the gates of Erebus, beneath
the Stygian city's wall, those monsters dwell,
the livid sisters. Their mother hides her coffers
in murky caves, and guzzles with dry throat
gold poured from a thousand refining fires,
nor can it sate the ardor of her thirst.
PRIDE towers in derision over all
the rest, scorning with blazing face her equal.
LUST lies submerged in burning slime, and writhes
with flames that ring her private parts, scorched to
the marrow. DRUNKENNESS grows nauseated,
while lavish GLUTTONY licks her own limbs,
and in her poverty consumes them. ANGER,
forgetful of herself, runs drunkenly
where impulse leads, scourging her fellows and
herself. BETRAYAL, TREACHERY's companion,
the daughter of gaunt ENVY, can't deny
what is well done, and yet by every means

assays its overthrow: she lessens praise
when to withdraw it is outside her power.
HYPOCRISY with livid, withered gaze
extols these mighty ones, and FLATTERY's plague,
today the highest road to courtly favor,
instills a venom lethal to the soul
with zeal into the greedy ears of princes:
such power is granted to this vice at court,
that it deprives lords of their human ears.
The First Parent of things passed by all these,
transfixing them with sidelong glance, and came
within the city walls, where she saw burning
the spirits in eternal crucibles.

[58] Sloping into the farthest cave of Hell,
a place lies where Gehenna's vengeful flame
doles endless punishment to guilty souls;
yet though a single flame torments them all,
the fires do not inflict one punishment,
but some are tortured less and others more.
Gehenna thus adapts to each one's merits,
that he who sinned less should know lesser pain,
while he should feel the fire more gravely, who
more gravely strayed. There are some whose lives knew
no blight, or venial, save for the flaw
of our first parent. On these the fiery mist
inflicts slight punishment, or none: just so,
in summer, when the noxious Dogstar scorches
the fields, beneath the same light of the sun
the sound man flourishes, the ill grows faint.
Leviathan stood there astride Hell's blast,
mingling the blazes of perpetual death,
when from afar he saw the goddess and
quit his furnace, coming forth to meet her.
Lest he should terrify her, serpent's guise
he laid aside. He took up once again
that first appearance which creating Nature
had given him, when, brighter than the sun,
he grew puffed up, and pride so swelled his mind
he sought to share Olympus' lofty heights.

[82] "Father of crimes, and their avenger," said
the goddess when she spied him, "you were cast
with hideous ruin and combustion down
from Heaven's citadel, for vainglory
of features that surpassed bright Lucifer.
Here, at last, in wretchedness I flee,
to you whom I received in earth's black night,
lest, lacking Heaven, you should have no throne.
I bring the shared complaints of gods and men
to you. You surely know with what great force
the elements are taxed by Alexander's
might at arms: when with his fleet he'd tamed
Pamphylia's sea, he conquered Darius thrice,
broke all of Asia, and compelled Porus,
unvanquished in all strife, to serve him. Nor
did that suffice, but now he traces out
the secrets of the East, and madly strikes
against Ocean itself. And if the Fates
should lend his sails kind winds, he plans to seek
the Nile's source, and lay siege to Paradise.
Look to yourself, or else he'll not permit
the hidden reaches of the Antipodes,
or deep Chaos itself, to go unscathed,
but strive to gaze upon the other sun.
Go then and smite our mutual pestilence.
What praise is yours, serpent, what glory, that
you cast the first man out, if such a garden
should yield its honors up to Alexander?"
No further words detained her. Following after,
the other pledged his care in all events:
he swore to her he'd not desist, until
their common foe was plunged in Hell's thick darkness.

[108] Without delay, he roused the shadowy town
and called a council, bellowing across
the ancient plain of evils, which there lay
hardened by ice, and ravaged by the snows,
unconquered by the sun or gentle breeze.
Here untold death tormented wicked souls
on every side: their thwarted will to die

itself was death. Since in this world, their life
lay dead with guilt, their death shall ever live
in punishment, that he who never ceased
to sin while living may not know the end,
there, of his dying. Miserable fate!
Smitten by ice and snow, they pass on thence
from cold to brimstone. Never and always
he dies, who suffers in Avernus' prison.
Here, when the gathered satraps of the Styx
and shadowy lords had found their wonted seats,
the ancient serpent stilled their murmuring
by hissing three times from his raucous throat:
the penalties of Hell compelled their silence,
and forced the shades to leave their grave laments.
[126] Rising when he had checked his breast's deep groans,
he set forth in their midst the goddess' will,
and added, "O comrades, what boundary,
what limit will encompass such a scourge,
before whom all things tremble, if delay
grants him more license to shatter the world?
But lo, I have kept silence—he prepares
to pierce earth's barriers, and, warring down
the masters of the shades, to penetrate
Tartarean Chaos, and lead forth its thralls.
Still is that fated which I loathe to tell:
a time shall come when some New Man, brought forth
by some great novelty upon the earth,
will overturn the pillars, and will break
the iron cloisters: seizing stronger arms,
he'll ravage with triumphal wood our halls.
Therefore, O lords of death, oppose this plague
nascent within the Macedonian king.
Lest he perchance prove victor over Hell,
cut off his life by sudden lethal stroke."
[143] He scarcely had belched out these words, when Treachery
arose with sly, alluring countenance,
and said: "Shortest of labors, this. I have
a venom deadlier than other draughts.
No pot will hold it, neither brazen jar,

nor glass, nor any other vessel, save
the nail of horse's hoof. To Alexander
this liquor, mingled with Falernian wine,
I'll give—and the occasion lies to hand:
for my Antipater, commander of
the Macedonian ranks, has feigned his love,
as taught since he lay bawling in his cradle,
yet in his marrow he conceals his hate.
Summoned to Babylon and to the king,
he hastens there to spend his latter days
beneath his rule, and once more to endure
the wrack of martial life, although a veteran.
If none among the night-born goddesses
holds wider sway than I, if you acknowledge
me as your foster daughter, I'll ascend
to higher regions, and by this man's hand
administer the poison to the duke."
Thus she spoke, and all the darkling host
as one acclaimed her plan. The entire council
praised her for zealous foresight, in preparing
to break with weaponed drink the one whom war
had left unbroken. Treachery straightway
now changed her ancient face, and left behind
the darkness, carried through Sicilian skies
on venomed wings. She came at length within
the secret chamber of her foster son,
whom she left well supplied with honeyed speech,
returning thence to seek her dwelling in
eternal Chaos, with its well-known shadows.

[168] Now Pella's hero with his threatening fleet
had broken the resistant Ocean, and
as victor over the indignant waves
prepared to go again to Babylon.
Unknowing of the future—wretched indeed!—
he undertook to carry forth his lances
toward Carthage, now that Asia was secure;
and passing thence through the Numidian lands,
he'd seek out Spain, where Hercules' pillars

were said to stand. From there, he'd pass all bounds
to subjugate the setting sun in war.
His thirsting soul conceived a daring plan
to cross the Pyrenees amidst such conquest,
and, mastering by arms the rebel Gauls,
to join Rhine's waters to the vanquished realms;
at last, he'd seek again his native land.
He'd cast aside en route the hindering Alps,
compelling Italy to serve him, and
would teach Rome to endure the Grecian yoke.
Therefore the Syrian prefects were enjoined
to seek material and to build a fleet:
now Lebanon bemoaned her cedars' height
laid headlong, the green alders there consigned
unto the waves: for that fleet her groves fell.
The earth gaped heavenward, deprived of her
arboreal tresses and perennial shade;
denuded peaks beheld the sun in wonder.
[191] Great One, where will your hunger lead? What end
will come of grasping? Pray, what bounds are set
unto your search? Where stands your labors' goal?
Madman, your works are naught. Though you enclose
all kingdoms in one empire, and subdue
the entire world, a pauper you remain
forever—for the soul is made a pauper
not by a dearth of wealth, but of contentment.
Even a little, if it would suffice,
will stave off want. But you, while gathering arms,
so well deceived, await a death prepared
by poison to repress those selfsame weapons!
His thirsty greed increases; yet one draught
will slake so great a thirst. For now Antipater,
the traitor, has arrived in Babylon,
flanked by his murderous accomplices,
imbued with shameful counsel, and conveyed
by wicked winds, to work that bitter outrage.
[205] O gods, O Fortune! What mad course is this?
Will you permit your scion's death, whom you

have so long shielded? If you cannot change
Fate's will that he of Macedon should die,
at least reveal these butchers' plot; replace
this with another death. You have the power:
exchange these agents of mortality,
exchange the poison for a sword. More fitly
he dies by arms, who by arms greatly erred.
Yet in plain light, perhaps, the gods could not
subdue the one whom surreptitious venom
could kill in secret; worthily, therefore
he falls by hidden crime, and no man's steel.

[216] Yet that this king of kings might see all realms
submitted to him, ere that final day
Fate had prepared, world ruler he was made
by dint of Fortune and by Fame's report.
Such terror and distress seized every race,
that after all the peoples of the East
had been subdued, the nations that remained
shook to the marrow. Every distant isle
felt fear, though girded by the surging main.
Descending to the sea and spreading sail,
from all the world came forth strange embassies
to bend the tyrant's course with proferred gifts.
The citadels of Carthage did not scorn
to lie beneath the Great One's sway, and likewise
all Africa sent word she was prepared
to serve the far-off Alexander. So
also wrote Spain, though mighty in her wars
and safely placed, constrained by fear alone,
while all of Gaul (this scarcely I'd believe)
revered the awful king and sent a diadem.
The madness of the Rhine grew mild: to Babylon
passed Teutons who had laid aside their rage,
alongside Flemish envoys, while no less
did dread compel the tribes of Italy.
Though nature had on one side placed the snows
of mountain peaks, and safe the land remained
upon the other, where the sea stood guard,
that country held no race invincible

before the Great One; of her own accord
she stemmed the king's wrath by a grant of tribute,
and Sicily declared her fiery peaks
and hellish lakes would serve the son of Philip.
What more to tell? All nations as though one
sought on the sea the towers of Semiramis.
There might you see legations flowing, ships
all laden with their varied stores and herds,
from places shifting Fame's loquacious breeze
you scarcely could have thought had ever reached.
[249] When Alexander heard a frightened world
had come together to check his advance,
he burned to see the place where he would die,
and, hastening the oars of his swift fleet,
made course for the city of Semiramis.
No otherwise, the tiger sees far off
a herd of horses, and a bitter thirst
burns in her flashing jaws; then is she lashed
by hunger's goad to drink in living blood,
and savagely devours the shredded limbs;
but if, perchance, upon a hidden path
the tracking hunter's spear pierces her flank,
she wails, her blood poured out, and dies upon
the grass, still thirsting, still unslaked with gore.
[260] Flanked by a guarding phalanx, now Pellaeus
enters—alas! those fatal citadels,
where, lo, a throng in splendid raiment shines
along his path. The princes come before him.
Among their numbers, proudly he goes in
to take up royal emblems in the city,
and orders the legations be admitted.
The monarch then ascends a throne, and from
the conquered world as conqueror receives
the tribute sent him: a gem-encrusted shield
from Gaul; a Carthaginian helmet blazing
with carbuncle at its peak; the Teuton's sword,
which seems to thirst for gore; from Spain a mount
with limbs of varied hue and foaming lips,
that chews the golden bridle's worn-down curb.

A close-linked coat of mail worked by the Cyclops
comes as the gift of the Sicilian tyrant.
[275] And still aside from these, as many diadems
as there were realms throughout the world marked him
as king of kings. Whatever could be found
to bring delight to gaze of mortal eyes,
enticement to the mind, from everywhere
was added to these trophies: purple robes
woven in wondrous fashion, varied garb
of divers nations, splendid ores and gems.
The wealth of all the world, in short, was heaped,
and when he had received such gifts, "Thanks be,"
he said, "unto the gods, by whose favor
all realms are made my due, along with cities
that still we have not seen. No less from you
are thanks due heaven, that apart from strife
of battle, without payment of your blood,
you've yielded to our reign and did not try
the strength of Macedon in close combat.
Had Darius humbly laid aside his crown,
surrendering himself, we'd have received
him in a portion of his realms, and nothing
would have seemed easier than this our yoke.
Take Porus as example of how mildly
I rule as victor over vanquished foes—
much more over the willingly compliant.
It is my will that every mortal passing
unconstrained by force beneath our yoke
should live in liberty, as though it were not
servitude, but liberty, to serve me.
Without distinction let one liberty
unite all those rebellion has not tainted."
[299] When thus he'd briefly spoken to the embassies,
he turned to those whose excellent virtue
had bowed down all the world. So he began:
"A prize awaits you, too, whose ardent toil
has left the world silent before our gaze.
That knight is worthy of me as his king—
—and I as king am worthy, too, of him—

whom winter did not chill on glacial shores,
nor Libya's raging heat reduce to slackness.
The Macedonian ranks beheld the sands
of Indic deserts mourn that by your forces
their prodigies were quelled. Why call to mind
our threefold triumph over Darius,
Mennon cast down, the arms of Taxiles
and Porus? Shall I speak of shapeless Giants
who yielded to you? Now that in this world
naught's left to finish, let us seek the peoples
who gaze upon the Antipodes' other sun;
let not our glorious arms fail to assay
whatever might increase them, or win odes
of endless song. No land will lie untrodden,
while I remain to lead my men. Toil conquers
all things, and nothing blocks the brave man's path.
The ancients teach us that more worlds exist;
alas, that I have yet to vanquish one!
Indeed, you know, comrades, how Rome once sent
the kingdom's diadem, writing to me
as to her king; yet now in broken faith,
her pride renewed, she violates the treaty
with obstinate countenance. So, first of all,
it pleases me to lay Rome waste, that no
perfection of my titles may be wanting,
nor any portion of this world escape
your triumphs." Having finished thus his speech,
he sent away the council, when already
the car of Phoebus had attained its goal.

[330] By now those fiery wheels had plunged the sun
beneath the thundering surges of the sea,
and headlong night had mingled all the elements
in her black sphere; now the nocturnal air
in sadness checked the stars, which strove to rise
and show their light. Advancing cloud and mist
repressed the constellations and the moon,
which should have held its sway in darkened hours.
The mariner, who sought the lesser Bear
and its companion Wain, which cannot sink

beneath the sea, lay helpless on that night:
his aimless prow adrift amidst the deep,
he dared nowhere to turn his starless course.
In presage of that coming death, all things
mourned Alexander's fate. Olympus wept
for one so soon to die, whose birth it had
portended with such noted signs as these:
real stones fell from the heavens, and in Egypt
a lamb spoke. A hen brought forth a dragon,
and—unless the rabble's hearsay feigns
truthful report—the day the queen gave birth,
above his father's roof paired eagles battled
like ordered squadrons. Prodigies so numerous
presaged his birth. What crime, O gods above,
in his brief lifetime lost for him your favor?
But if he'd been content with mortal honor,
if in the midst of all prosperity
he'd shown humble comportment, and had borne
alike the sweet and bitter fruits of Fortune,
perhaps by Fate he still might have evaded
both sword and poison crueler than the sword.
[356] Sluggard Boötes turned his long-spent cart.
Night's candles were burnt out, and jocund day
had lulled the shadows with its infant light.
But yet the dewy humor of the dawn
did not fall on the grass as the light rose,
nor birds anticipate the day with song
harmonious beneath the trembling frond.
The nightingale, foreknowing grief to come,
suppressed the lute of her love-laden voice;
they say that Lucifer gave place to day
while yet the other stars refused to yield.
Reversing his accustomed path, the Titan
first bent a low course toward the sea's west edge;
but from the Nabataean waves unwillingly,
no longer able to delay the Fates,
at last he reared his ray-surrounded head:
had not Fate's clear-known sequence blocked his path,
he threatened to turn back his carriage-beam

with all his strength. Parent of light and fire,
O stay your course, revered one, stay your course!
Your lamp, O Phoebus, if you fail to turn
aside your orb of light, will quench the lamp
of all the teeming Macedonian host.

[375] But now had come the fatal hour, in which
that master, great of heart, would be cast down.
The Fates would brook no further hesitation,
but sped that crime of universal ruin.
Redolent with the perfumes of the East,
the hall shone brightly where the people and
the princes' sacred order had assembled.
A great part of the day had been consumed
in speeches, and the duke had doled out treasure,
enriching all, when brimming cups of wine
were borne at his command unto the ministers.
And thus, as lord and father among friends
he perished, who so often had laid waste
the foe's prowess and yet emerged unscathed.

[386] His body stiffened with a sudden torpor.
His knees grew slack; his limbs he scarce could master,
and so upon a bed they laid him. All
the palace shook at once with mortal tumult,
though still none dared to show the grief he felt,
in hope that Fortune's remedy might yet
be near at hand—for she had stood beside him
on all occasions, when he chanced to fall.
But when the poison had imbued his veins,
and when his pulse gave signs of coming death,
he ordered that his bed be laid in hall.
There, once the frantic army had assembled,
the noble band of dukes, commingled with
the common rank and file, he gazed upon them
scoring their faces, eyes awash with tears.
"Where shall such men attain a worthy king,"
he said, "when I depart the earth? Enough
it is for me, that I have ruled the world.
All favorable chance beneath the stars
has come to me compliantly in warfare.

No longer am I pleased to be confined
by mortal frame. I've spent my allotted season
consumed by human cares, and long enough
I've tarried, thus, till now, among mere mortals.
Henceforth to greater matters am I summoned.
High heaven itself calls me to rule Olympus;
there, having gained my seat and royal throne
among the stars, with Jove I shall dispose
the secrets of all things, and give my judgments
of men's brief outcomes and the gods' affairs.
Perhaps presumption arms once more those brothers
buried at Etna, and Pelorus' ridge
has loosed Typhoeus' savage limbs against
the gods' host and their lofty citadels.
They think the gods and stars can easily
be taken from a senile Jove; again
they mount their challenge, and since Mars himself
without me flees the danger of the fray,
I'm summoned, though resistant and unwilling,
by counsel of great Jove and of the gods,
to a new realm." When he had spoken thus,
with lamentation and with flowing tears
they pressed forward, to ask whom he desired
to leave as heir and ruler of the world.
"The best," he said, "and worthiest of power
shall be your king." But afterward no voice
remained to him. Then, drawing from his finger
a golden ring, to Perdicas he gave it,
and so the dukes supposed the king desired
that Perdicas succeed him in the realm.
Immediately, the warmth of life departed
the corpse, now slack with cold; and, breaking forth
from its prison of clay, the spirit passed
into thin air. Then from their grief was loosed
the bitterest of mourning; lamentation
broke in all its strength, nor did the crowd
further suppress its fearful tumult. Such
a crashing does not press against the stars,

when, hurling thunder, the four brother winds
strike at the pole of heaven and its lights.
[433] O happy race of mortals, if at all times
we might consider the eternal Good,
might fear the end which, though unseen, approaches
for nobleman and commoner alike.
We search out wealth in peril of our souls;
around our mortal eyes deceitful glory
of action flies on wings of vanity.
In grasping at those honors now for sale,
we scour the sea's billows, and in hatred
of our own lives, unto the tumid surge
commit our persons and our goods. Perchance
through Alpine winters and a horde of thieves
we strive to reach the walls of greedy Rome,
and Romulus' citadels: if by some chance
we come again to our ancestral land
and native soil, the onset of a slight
and sudden fever scatters all we've gathered
in all our years. Thus will the Great One serve
as an example. Five feet of carved stone
sufficed for his abode in tunneled earth,
for whom the world held insufficient space.
The noble corpse there rested in scant soil,
until that remnant of dread Fate, honored
by all the world, was moved by Ptolemy—
to whom you read that Egypt fell as lot—
into that town which he named for the prince.
[455] But now the sun's about to plunge his gaze
in headlong night; he steers his breathless chariot
towards the sea. Now is it all played out,
now comes the time to end the game. O Muses,
hereafter other souls may be enticed
by your sweet strains. I seek another fount:
once drunk, it remedies a second thirst.
[461] But you, whose full-horned bounty has poured out
your wealth upon me, that I might despise
the tongues of enemies, receive, O great

prelate, the zealous labor of your Walter.
Do not disdain to join around your brow
the poet's ivy to the sacred mitre.
For though this song may be unworthy of
so great a bishop, yet when spirit passes
from mortal limbs, together we shall live.
Surviving with his poet, William's glory
shall live undying through all time to come.

Notes

Quotation marks around a note indicate that I have translated it from a medieval gloss in a surviving manuscript of the *Alexandreis*. The shelfmark of the manuscript then follows in parentheses. When parentheses enclose a single capital letter, a Latin text of the gloss can be found on pp. 275–514 of Colker's edition of the poem (G=Geneva, Bibliothèque Publique et Universitaire MS lat. 98; C=Erfurt, Wissenschaftliche Bibliothek MS Amplon. 8° 17; V=Vienna, Österreichische Nationalbibliothek MS 568; R=Rome, Bibliotheca Apostolica Vaticana MS lat. 1479).

Prologue

well-turned verses: Walter here borrows a metaphor from Horace's *Ars poetica*, line 441. Horace's discursive poem on poetic composition was among the best-known works of classical literary theory during the central Middle Ages.

the bard of Mantua: Vergil.

Jerome: Born about 345, Jerome translated Scripture into the Vulgate Latin version canonical throughout Western Europe. A master of late classical prose style, he was also a contentious refuter of his theological and ecclesiastical rivals.

Servius: Servius Maurus Honoratus, a fourth-century commentator on the works of Vergil. Servius in fact nowhere makes such a statement.

chapter headings: By declaring his authorship of the ten lines of verse summary that preface each book of the poem in most manuscripts, Walter reinforces the sense, built up in the prologue as a whole, that he intends his poem to become a lasting addition to the literary canon, and so an object of serious scrutiny. One might compare other examples of the authorially annotated poem, for instance Gower's *Confessio Amantis*, or closer to our own day, Eliot's *The Waste Land*.

Book One

1.1. *Duke of Macedon*: In classical epic usage, *dux* often simply denotes a military commander; but in a twelfth-century text as read in the thirteenth and fourteenth centuries, a more feudal sense of *dux* suggests itself, just as in Shakespeare Theseus has become "Duke of Athens." *Dux Macedum* appears throughout the poem as an epithet for Alexander, as do *Pellaeus*, i.e., "one from Pella," Alexander's birthplace, and *Macedo*, simply "the Macedonian."

1.16. *whose royal forebears Britain vaunts*: Walter's patron and dedicatee, William of the White Hands, was great-grandson of William the Conqueror and uncle of King Philip Augustus of France. Earlier bishop of Chartres and then archbishop of Sens, he was consecrated archbishop of Reims in 1176.

1.18. *Brennius*: "He touches upon how, under Brennius' leadership, the men of Sens advanced on Rome even as far as the Capitol; but the watchmen were roused by a goose, and so they repelled Brennius and his comrades." (V) Livy recounts this episode from the siege of Rome by the Gauls in 390 B.C.E. in Book 5.47.

1.23–24. *any earlier name for harshness*: "Because at first the city had been called Duricordium." (V) That is, Walter plays here on the Latin for "hard-heartedness"; the classical form, from Caesar's *Gallic Wars* 6.44.1, is "Durocortorum."

1.26. *Helicon*: "Helicon is the mount upon which dwell the Muses, but here it is used as a substitute for 'wisdom.'" (C)

1.32. *pour out the holy waters*: "This is adapted from the ancients, who are said to have gained their teachings or knowledge from the fountain of Pegasus." (C)

1.49. *Hercules*: "Jupiter begat Hercules from Alcmena, wife of Amphitryon. But Amphitryon begat from her Iphiclus. Juno, wishing to learn which of them was Jove's son, sent two serpents. Iphicles fled when he saw them. But Hercules throttled them, and so it was known which was Jove's son." (V)

1.52. *Aristotle's name*: Aristotle served as tutor to the young Alexander, a circumstance that contributed significantly to the Alexander tradition by supplying the fictive pretext for several works, including *The Letter of Alexander to Aristotle* and the *Secret of Secrets*. Walter cannot have known the latter in its full form, but he must have had some access to a partial version of the text, which was first translated from Syriac into Latin in the twelfth century, since on it he loosely based the advice to Alexander that follows in lines 100–216.

1.59. *Nectanabus*: "Nectanabus was a most learned astrologer and king of Egypt, but he left Egypt of his own accord, since he knew he would be driven out if he joined battle with his enemies. He came to Greece and there deceived Olympias, wife of King Philip, by his magic arts. From her he begat Alexander, by whom he was struck down while he was tutoring him in astrology." (G) The legend of Alexander's illegitimate parentage, drawn from the *Historia de preliis*, is occasionally but not frequently mentioned by Walter; Walter's Alexander expresses intermittent anxieties about his lineage.

1.97. *the stuff of virtue*: Walter's Aristotle begins his long passage of advice by deploying some of the central categories of Aristotelian thought as assimilated in the twelfth-century schools, viz., the concepts of form and matter, potentiality and actuality.

1.206. *Astraea*: The goddess of justice, Astraea departed the earth at the end of the Golden Age: Ovid, *Metamorphoses*, 1.150.

1.246. *its idols cast out*: Acts 18.

1.260. *Nestor*: "Nestor, that is wisdom, conceded to Achilles, that is, to fortitude." (C)

1.279. *the month whose name's derived from youth*: "The month of June [*Iunius*] takes its name from young men [*iuuenibus*], because in that month youths give themselves up to youthful games." (R) The penchant for etymologization ran deep in medieval literary culture, thanks in large measure to Isidore of Seville's sixth-century encyclopedia, the *Etymologies*. In Latin verse, circumlocution by etymology sometimes afforded a way around the metrical irregularity of necessary proper names and technical terms, as at 7.356.

1.317. *Demosthenes*: The preeminent Athenian orator advocated armed opposition to Alexander in his *Philippics*. His rival Aeschines argued for a policy of cooperation.

1.322. *safe in Pallas' citadel*: "Because Athens was divided into three parts, to wit, the port, which was consecrated to Neptune, and the quarter of Pallas, where the soldiers and men of war resided, and the Areopagus, that is the quarter in which resided the student clerks." (V)

1.347. *the whole race stood accused*: "Because Cadmus slew the serpent which had killed his companions, whom he had sent to seek water after he found a place to establish a city. He sowed its teeth; from them armed men sprang up who killed one another. Some also helped him to found the city. Niobe compared herself to Latona in beauty. Latona then reported this to her son Phoebus. He killed the woman's seven sons, and Diana her seven daughters, and she was turned to stone. Agave, who was unwilling to sacrifice to Bacchus, dismembered her own son Pentheus while she was drunk. Juno, in the guise of an old woman, tricked Semele into asking Jove, with whom she was having an affair, to come to her as he came to Juno, that she might test his godhead; and she was thunderstruck by Jove. Oedipus killed his father and slept with his mother, from whom were born Eteocles and Polynices; they waged war for the kingdom when their father had died." (G)

1.399. *built by Amphion's sweet strains*: "The son of Antiopa. Amphion was the son of Jove, an excellent harpist, and king of Thebes." (G)

1.409. *Vulcan's stroke*: "That is, fire." (G)

1.410. *Dirce's fields*: "He touches on a fable: Dirce was the wife of Lycus; she was changed into a fountain of the same name near Thebes." (C)

1.459. *the third part of the world*: "The seventh heading, where he describes Asia on account of Alexander, as Lucan describes Libya on account of Cato. Asia, then, is the third part of the world in number, not quantity: its length extends from north to south, its breadth from the east as far as Europe, and there it is bounded by the Mediterranean Sea, in the north by Tanais and Maeotis, on the east by Ocean, on the south by the Nile, whence it comprises as much as Europe and Africa. Hence Asia is named for the queen who ruled it, as Europe is named for Europa, daughter of Agenor." (C) On the vast subject of medieval geography and mapmaking as it relates to the *Alexandreis*, see Maura K. Lafferty, "Mapping Human Limitations: The Tomb Ecphrases in Walter of Châtillon's *Alexandreis*," *Journal of Medieval Latin* 4 (1994), 64–81, esp. 73–81. In the so-called T-O map, the earth is schematically represented by a circle bisected by a horizontal diameter. Above this line lies Asia; Europe and Africa make up the lower left and right quarters, respectively, divided by a radius drawn to the bottom of the circle. Jerusalem stands at the circle's center. The elaborate and monumental maps of the thirteenth century, for example the Ebstorf and Hereford Maps, begin with this basic schema but refine it enormously. Rudimentary T-O maps appear in some *Alexandreis* mansucripts as a gloss to the present passage. World geography as understood in Walter's day will again come to the fore in the ecphrasis of Darius' tomb at 7.420–77.

1.464. *Lake Maeotis and the Tanais*: In modern parlance, the Sea of Azov and the Don.

1.486. *the Phoenix*: This self-immolating and resurrecting bird was one of a kind. Hence we find manuscript glosses on *despair of all logicians* of the following sort: "Logicians argue whether the proposition 'Every Phoenix is . . .' can be true and possible, since 'every' is a distributive universal, and that bird is always one." (R)

1.490. *Armenia*: "The very high land in which Noah's ark rested after the Flood." (R)

1.531. *broken faith*: "Because Laomedon promised Phoebus a basket of gold for building the walls of Troy. He afterwards denied this, and so broke faith." (C)

1.533. *wingèd Jove*: "Jupiter in the form of an eagle carried off Ganymede, who afterward became Jove's cup bearer." (C)

1.538. *Oenone's poplar*: "Paris and Oenone tended flocks in the forest of Ida. Paris loved her and knew her and wrote on a tree by the river Xanthus, 'If Paris still shall breathe when he has scorned Oenone, Xanthus' stream shall flow reversed,' as it appears in Ovid's *Heroides* [5.29–30]." (V)

1.542. *the case was tried*: "He touches on the story of how Paris judged Venus more beautiful; but this is such a well-known tale that it is unnecessary to record it here." (V)

1.563. *Maeonia's bard*: Homer.

1.572–73. *Atlas and the Ganges . . . Boreas and Ammon*: The west, east, north, and south, respectively.

1.590. *when Pausanias had paid his debt*: As the murderer of Alexander's father, Philip.

1.610. *twelve gemstones*: The details of the figure's appearance mark him clearly as the Hebrew High Priest, or as God in the guise of the High Priest; the four unrecognized characters on his brow are the tetragrammaton, the letters of the Divine Name (YHWH).

Book Two

2.30. *I send you gifts more suited to your age*: This scene, which derives ultimately from the Greek Alexander romance of Pseudo-Callisthenes, comes to figure as a topos in other tales of young rulers of great promise insulted by complacent older monarchs. The most famous example is Shakespeare's *Henry V*, Act I, Scene 2, where the young Henry rebuffs the emissaries of the King of France, who have presented him with a gift of tennis balls. See Judith Mossman, "*Henry V* and Plutarch's *Alexander*," *Shakespeare Quarterly* 45 (1994), 59–60.

2.52. *Mennon's death*: With this allusion, Walter skips over the first encounter between Alexander and Darius' forces. In lines 72 ff. he returns to it briefly.

2.62. *according to the example set by Xerxes*: "Xerxes was a king with so large an army that he could not count it. Finally, he ordered each man to shoot one arrow toward a single spot, and so he knew his men's number when the arrows were gathered. Darius likewise commanded each of his men to cast a lance or shaft, and so he counted his soldiers." (V)

2.69. *Baucis*: "That is, a little old woman, a proper name being substituted here for a common noun. According to the fable, she was the wife of Philemon. They offered hospitality to the gods, at whose order their house was transformed into a temple [*Metamorphoses* 8.626–724]." (G)

2.70. *Faunus*: "the god of goats." (G)

2.84. *Here in Jove's temple*: "Gordias was a soldier who one day while walking in a field was surrounded by countless birds. Marveling at this, he left the field to ask the sages what it might mean. A girl met him on his way and asked him what he was seeking. Gordias told her everything. She said. 'This means that you will rule all Asia.' Gordias therefore rejoiced and took her to wife. When the king of Asia died, the princes gathered to choose a king, and they agreed in deliberation to crown whatever man was sitting in a chariot when he met them. Gordias met them and so was made king. Afterward he begat Midas. Midas, in honor of that chariot in which his father had sat when he was made king, made a golden car, which he tied in the temple of Jove with countless fated knots, and it was destined that whoever loosed those knots would rule in Asia. One day Alexander entered the temple of Jove and tried to loosen the knot and was unable to untie it with his hands. Seeing this, he seized a sword and cut through the middle. It is this of which the author is speaking." (V)

2.126. *whom vulgar error called Immortals*: The conceit is that, since their numbers were maintained at a constant level, one could imagine that none ever died.

2.164. *Tarsus*: "At Tarsus was born the blessed Paul, who converted many to the catholic faith." (V)

2.187. *the spirit found his arteries all blocked*: "Note that pores are tiny openings in a man, which are dilated by sweat. In Alexander they were opened by heat, and so cold entered Alexander's body all the more easily since they were opened, whence it happened that he grew ill. 'Arteries' are veins of pulsation, which were constricted in Alexander, or else arteries are the openings of the throat, to wit the jaws. . . . Alexander's spirit had no free egress through them, and so he grew infirm." (V)

2.198. *Tesiphone*: "An infernal Fury, that is, the Devil." (V)

2.209. *she sat and turned her wheel*: The personified Goddess Fortuna is one of the most ubiquitous figures in medieval literature, largely due to Boethius' immensely influential *Consolation of Philosophy*. See F.P. Pickering, *Literature and Art in the Middle Ages* (London: Macmillan, 1970), chap. 3.

2.259. *his Archigenes*: His doctor. The name given him here is figurative: it is that of a physician who appears in Juvenal 6.236, 13.98, and 14.252.

2.360. *Mother Cybele*: "Cybele is the goddess of the earth, or the earth itself. Flora is the goddess of flowers, but Cybele is here said to wed Zephyrus to Flora, goddess of flowers, because Zephyrus is the lightest of winds, at whose breath flowers grow." (V)

2.364–65. *where Maximian slew Eastern troops*: "He shows by the comparison how that spring descends. He says that it descends as the Rhône descends from the Alps. Next to that river, blessed Mauritius and his companions were slain by Maximian. Maximian was the prefect of Diocletian, Emperor of Rome. The Romans dispatched this Maximian against a tyrant of Cisalpine Gaul who was harrying the Roman Empire, and under Maximian were dispatched blessed Mauritius and his companions. But when Maximian had crossed the Alps, he ordered his men to sacrifice to idols. Blessed Mauritius and his companions would not obey, saying that they adored the one God. When Maximian had heard this, he ordered certain very noble men killed. When, after this, they still would not celebrate the worship of idols, he commanded every tenth man in their whole column to be killed. But when he saw that a contention rose among them over who would receive the glory of martyrdom, he ordered them all to be killed, and the inundation of their blood swelled the river's flow."(V)

2.379. *the veneration of a holy idol*: "That is, a sacred image. Note that Nimrod begat Belus, and Belus Ninus. Ninus made for the dead Belus an image in the likeness of his father, to which he paid such reverence that he would spare all men who fled to it, and so men of his kingdom began to pay divine honors to the image. Some call this image Bel, others Baal, others Belial, others Beelzebub, that is, 'the lord of the flies,' others Beelphegor." (C)

2.394. *the River Granicus*: "Where Alexander sustained losses when he fought, for many of his soldiers were killed; and yet he gained the victory." (C)

2.407. *that we trace back our lineage to the Giants*: "Note that in Babylon demons entered the bodies of women, whence Giants like Nimrod and many others were born. Of their stock were born Darius and Belus and Darius' other ancestors."(V) (Such traditions go back, through Augustine's *City of God*, to Genesis 6.1–4.)

2.410. *the Tower*: Genesis 11.

2.467. *Lycaon*: "That is, a wolf. He alludes to the fable of Lycaon, and it is an urbane substitution when a proper noun is substituted for a common." (V) The story of Lycaon's transformation is found in Ovid, *Metamorphoses* 1.221–39.

2.511. *the sharer of his secrets*: "Because together they committed the vice of Sodom. Or else, *the sharer* of other secret matters, and better so according to the author's intention, since in this book the author conceals those matters which ought to be concealed." (V)

2.560. *the crimes of Xerxes*: I.e., in invading Greece during the Persian War in 480 B.C.E.

2.573. *disembodied Echo*: Ovid, *Metamorphoses* 3.358–61.

2.575. *Darius' arms*: The first of the poem's three ecphrases, or formal descriptions of artifacts, the Shield of Darius is accorded particularly dense commentary in some of the surviving manuscripts. Other such densely glossed passages include the appearance of the High Priest at the end of Book One, Alexander's combat with Zoroas in Book Three, and the ecphrasis on the tomb of Darius' wife in Book Four. The subject matter of the Shield is almost entirely biblical, as is that of the tomb of Darius' wife. The passage's most important antecedent in classical literature is the description of the arms of Aeneas at the end of *Aeneid* 7, itself an emulation of the shield of Achilles in the *Iliad*. The most important biblical references in the present passage include Genesis 6–11, 2 Kings 24–25, and Daniel 4–5 and 9. On Croesus and Apollo, see the note on 5.453 below.

Book Three

3.161. *Bellona*: The goddess of war.

3.169. *Zoroas of Memphis*: Zoroas, as a living repository of the quadrivium, attracted substantial attention from the poem's thirteenth- and fourteenth-century glossators. The passage shares many lines with a *prosimetrum* of Walter's dating from 1174–76. Carlotta Dionisotti, "Walter of Châtillon and the Greeks," in Peter Godman and Oswyn Murray, eds., *Latin Poetry and the Classical Tradition: Essays in Medieval and Renaissance Literature* (Oxford: Clarendon Press, 1990), 90–96, argues that the present version of the shared material is the earlier, and she dates the *Alexandreis* to the years 1171–76.

3.183. *the adverse Old Man*: "Saturn is called an old man because of his slow gait, since he progresses for thirty years through the Zodiac. Similarly, Diana or the moon is called a huntress because in a single month, as in a lesser space, she traverses the same Zodiac." (V)

3.187. *all human events*: "Thus it is understood that he was skilled in the art of magic. Magic includes five categories, to wit prophecy, conjuring, mathematics, witchcraft, and fortune-telling. Prophecy is understood as the knowledge of divine matters, and it has four categories, according to the four elements, and a fifth according to the dead below. The first is pyromancy, which derives from 'pyr,' which is fire, and 'manthos,' which is divination. The second category is aeromancy, which is practiced in the air, as when images result from the vibrations set up in the air by swords. The third is hydromancy, which is practiced in a basin filled with water. The fourth is geomancy, from 'geon,' earth. This is practiced at intersections, at forked and triple paths. The fifth is necromancy, from 'nigros,' which is death, because it is practiced with the bones of the dead and things of like sort. The second category of the art of magic as a whole is conjuring, to wit, when men make themselves invisible, or change themselves into pigs or birds or various other likenesses. Mercury invented this category of magic. The third category of the magic art is mathematics, which is named for 'mathesis,' protracted memory. . . . Under this there are three divisions, to wit haruspicy, horospicy, and auspicy. Haruspicy is when future events are discerned in the entrails of beasts, which of old were sacrificed at altars, and when they were slaughtered, the victims saw things to come. . . . Horospicy is divination according to the grades of the signs and the hours. . . . Auspicy has to do with birds, and again it has four divisions. . . . The fourth category of magic art is witchcraft, when future events are known through demons. The fifth and last category of the art of magic as a whole is fortune-telling, to wit, the knowledge of future events by lot. Of this there are many varieties, nor are they comprised under any fixed number, since there are various tellings of fortune among various individuals. And so when he says *sought their paths* [line 186], he notes that Zoroas was skilled in pyromancy; but when he adds *noted their hours* [line 187], he records that he was skilled in horospicy." (V)

3.205. *the ark of sevenfold wisdom*: "That is, having seven folds, that is, the seven liberal arts." (V)

3.393. *the spouse of Venus*: "That is, Vulcan" (C) (i.e., fire).

3.396. *poets' gleaming words*: "That is, Lucan's, who ascribes the invention of letters to the Tyrians, saying, 'If Fame we may believe, Phoenicians first dared give to rustic voices lasting shape.' Likewise Theodulus: 'Among the Greeks 'twas Cadmus first traced letters.' " (V)

3.402–403. *a populace of orthodox belief*: The Latin Kingdom of Jerusalem was established in 1099 and lasted until 1244. Walter's gesture here to the triumphalism of the Crusades foreshadows the end of Book Five; but there the celebration of the crusaders' New World Order is made problematic by the very association with Alexander's career has occasioned the excursus.

3.427. *ten years hence*: See 10.164–197.

3.509. *adultery's avenger*: "To wit, Menelaus, [avenger] of the adultery of Paris and Helen." (V)

3.510. *Aulis*: Iphigenia, daughter of Agamemnon, was sacrificed at Aulis by the priest Calchas to appease Artemis and thus to obtain a favorable wind for the Greek fleet on its way to the siege of Troy.

3.517. *No otherwise*: "By the simile he shows how Alexander marveled. . . . This Antaeus was a Giant who killed men. Hercules fought with him, and as often as Antaeus fell to the earth, he regained his strength and rose even stronger. Realizing this, Hercules was greatly amazed and raised him above his breast, saying, 'Here, Antaeus, you'll fall,' and so he forced him to die in mid-air." (V)

3.523. *the fecund Hydra*: "That is, a serpent whose nature was such that when one of its heads was cut off, two more grew, and so it was all the more powerful for its wounding. Hercules fought with it and was greatly amazed. At last he killed it." (V)

3.548. *Actaeon*: "Actaeon was changed into a stag, whence he substitutes 'Actaeon' for 'stag,' which is an elegant replacement." (V) Actaeon was transformed into a stag as a punishment from Diana; he was rent asunder by his own hounds (Ovid, *Metamorphoses* 3.137–252).

Book Four

4.86. *Athena's olive branch*: "Enemies were accustomed to carry an olive bough as a sign of peace."(C)

4.222–342. In the surviving medieval witnesses, this ecphrasis on the tomb of Darius' wife is the most heavily annotated single passage in the poem. A number of manuscripts, for example, London, British Library MS Burney 312 and Add. MS 30,071, carry a gloss "wrapped" around a text whose layout has been adjusted to allow for the full extent of the accompanying commentary. In others, for example British Library, Add. MS 18,217 and Oxford, Bodleian Library, Laud misc. 536, separate free-standing commentaries devoted solely to this passage follow the full text of the poem. For more on these glosses, and on the passage's significance for the poem's design, see David Townsend, "*Mihi barbaries incognita linguae*: Other Voices and Other Visions in Walter of Châtillon's *Alexandreis*," *Allegorica* 12 (1992), 22–23.

4.225. *the Jew Apelles*: Walter has conflated the historical sculptor of the fourth century B.C.E. with a Jew of the same name mentioned in Horace's Satires, 1.5.100. Walter also mentions him in his *Tractatus contra Iudaeos*, Patrologia Latina 209, col. 447.

4.229. *There Matter lay*: Walter gives to the creation story of Genesis 1 a cosmological inflection in keeping with the Neoplatonism of the so-called School of Chartres. See Winthrop Wetherbee, *Platonism and Poetry in the Twelfth Century: The Literary Influence of the School of Chartres* (Princeton, N.J.: Princeton University Press, 1972). "This is in agreement with Ovid, who says, 'Throughout the world all nature's face was one, a rude and unformed mass, which they called Chaos', etc. . . . The philosophers' opinions were various as to the creation and origin of things. Some, like Anaxagoras and Heraclitus, said that all things were brought forth from fire. In accordance with such men, Vergil says [*Aeneid* 6.394], 'The Father spoke, subdued by endless love.' Others like Mellissus said that it was brought forth from moisture, whence Vergil says [*Georgics* 4.382], 'And Ocean, father of all things.' Others like Empedocles said it was brought forth from four elements, and so Lucretius says [1.715], 'From rain and earth and fire all things were born.' But the Epicureans said that there were two principles of things, namely body and the void; for everything that is, either contains or is contained, whence the container is said to be the void, for example air, while that which is contained is body. They also said that bodies were atoms, to wit, those tiny bodies which are seen in sunbeams, so small that they are scarcely visible, while the void is that space in which the atoms exist. But according to true belief, the origin of all things is brought forth from four elements by the mediation of divine power, whence Vergil says: 'He sang how through the mighty void were driven the seeds of earth, of spirit, and of sea, and of the flowing fire, all things' beginnings; he held the world at birth, while still earth trembled.' Apelles, following this opinion, depicted four elements, of which all things were made." (V)

4.230. *in varied hue*: "That is, of a variety of hues. For we recognize fire by its redness, air by its whiteness, water by its greenness, and earth by its blackness. The fact that they have these colors makes the rainbow visible, which is informed by the properties of each of the elements. *Hyle* means 'timber,' since just as different materials can be made from limbs of trees, so from *hyle* many various creatures are divided and separated, whence Bernard Silvester [*Cosmographia* 1.2]: '*Hyle* is nature's most ancient face, undivided by any generation, the first subject of forms, the matter of bodies, the foundation of substance.' He also says of *hyle* [*Cosmographia* 1.1], 'Stiff timber, unformed Chaos, hostile mass, discolored face of being, and self-conflicted.' " (V)

4.231. *as it brought forth four elements*: "*Hyle* [Greek, "matter'] is said to bring forth four elements, which is easily understood in its specifics: for earth is cold and dry, air hot and moist. And so taking cold from the earth and moist from the air, water is produced, and so in regard to all the rest:

Fire	hot and dry
Air	hot and moist
Water	cold and moist
Earth	cold and dry" (V)

4.231–32. *each pressed with its own seal*: "In order to receive a form. He calls the elemental properties 'seals' of the elements, because just as a seal presses wax and shapes it, so also an elemental property shapes an element; or just as wax receives various figures by the seal's impression, so *hyle* receives various qualities which are called elements. . . ." (V)

4.243. *twice wed Lamech*: according to an exegesis that derives ultimately from rabbinic tradition, the young man slain by Lamech in Genesis 4:16–24 was Cain himself (Peter Comestor, *Historia scholastica* PL 198, col. 1079).

4.252. *vineyards are planted*: Genesis 9:20–27. "Noah was the first to plant vines, and drinking the wine and not knowing its power, he became drunk, and while sleeping he was uncovered around his manly organs or *pudenda*: so it is clear that men still wore no loincloths or breeches. Thus

Ham, seeing his father's testicles, laughed and told his brothers, one of whom ran to cover him with his cloak, whence the verse 'As Ham laughed at his father's parts' uncovering, the Jews mocked God's own death amidst his suffering.' " (V)

4.256. *Jacob comes again*: Genesis 32:7, 24.

4.258. *Joseph's abduction*: Genesis 37–50.

4.265. *Ben-Nun*: Joshua.

4.280. *From Benjamin comes forth a man*: Saul, of the tribe of Benjamin.

4.286. *the king's curse rages*: 2 Samuel 1.

4.287. *Asahel and Abner*: 2 Samuel 2–3.

4.287. *Uriah*: 2 Samuel 11.

4.289. *the patricide*: 2 Samuel 18.

4.292. *the Peaceful*: Solomon.

4.294. *Joab*: 1 Kings 2.

4.296. *unending schism*: 1 Kings 12.

4.303. *Jezebel*: 2 Kings 9.

4.304. *the death of Ahab*: 1 Kings 22.

4.304. *the blood-bought vines*: 1 Kings 21.

4.305. *the fifty*: 2 Kings 1.

4.307. *Baal's sacred throng*: 1 Kings 18.

4.308. *the disciple cannot find his master*: 2 Kings 2.

4.311. *Hezekiah*: 2 Kings 18–20.

4.314. *Josiah*: 2 Kings 23.

4.320. *to Ahaz a sign is granted*: Isaiah 7:10–14.

4.323. *the city's fall*: Jeremiah 31.

4.328. *a long-closed gate*: Ezechiel 44:1–3.

4.330. *Daniel prophesies*: Daniel 9:24–27.

4.335–36. *Zorababel leads them*: Ezra 5.

4.338. *Haman's death*: Esther 6–7.

4.339. *Vashti's haughtiness*: Esther 1

4.339–40. *Here sits Tobias*: Tobit 2.

4.341. *manly Judith*: Judith 13.

4.342. *with Ezra*: "Ezra, who came of the line of Aaron, restored the law burned by the Chaldeans and devised new letters which were easier to write and pronounce, and thereafter he was called a prophet. And here we read *the picture's sequence*, etc., as if he were to say: the register of kings and patriarchs has its end in Ezra, that is, in the prophet who lived under King Artaxerxes, the predecessor of Darius. And, not to seem to digress unnecessarily, it must be noted that on the tombs of nobles were depicted the deeds of their own race and their own deeds. Ovid suggests this when he says, 'Amidst the city's panoply of statues, her father stood, magnificent of titles' [*Heroides* 2.67–8]; and in Lucan, 'But if you deem stone worthy of that name, add too such mighty deeds, his greatest monuments' [8.806–7]. Alexander therefore had the race of Darius' wife represented, and the deeds of that race, according to its nobility, or rather with an eye to the declaration of his own praise, to wit, in order to commemorate his victory, or else to spread report of his piety and humanity. For he behaved toward his enemies as Caesar and other kings did toward friends, as is clear in Lucan. Moreover, this woman was noble, descending from Adam by a long line through the patriarchs, judges, kings, and prophets; and the names of each order are recorded, first the patriarchs, second the judges, third the kings, fourth the prophets, as can be seen above."(V) The interest shown by this gloss in the spatial arrangement of the iconographical program is paralleled by a gloss in BL Add. MS 23,891: "The tomb was decorated in five zones. In the first was the order of the patriarchs, as is clear from the passage where he says *the sequence of the patriarchs*. In the second was contained the stories which are in Exodus, as is evident in the passage *Here Egypt grieves*. In the third, the order of judges, as is evident in the passage *the judges' rule*. In the fourth zone, the order of kings, as we see in the passage *a new division*. And in the fifth and last, the order of the prophets, as we see in the passage *the prophets' images*. Hence the verses, 'Apelles' tomb stands pictured in five bands—first patriarchs, then Exodus here stands. The third the judges' deeds, the fourth the kings; the prophets then come last of all these things.'" One might note that in this latter gloss, which takes the trouble to provide mnemonic verses, the iconographical scheme is conceived in five divisions, rather than in the four of the gloss from the Vienna manuscript.

4.389. *Typhus*: "An urbane substitution of proper for common noun. He shows by the simile how fearful Alexander was: just as a sailor who sails through the sea in favorable winds has recourse to the assistance of the oars if a storm should overwhelm him, so Alexander, driven to fear by what he had seen, fled from such a multitude of Persians to his soldiers, seeking what should be done." (V)

4.536. *Lethe's liquor*: "Lethe is a marsh in Hell which brings on oblivion. Similiarly, those who sleep are in oblivion." (V)

4.544. *the Hyperborean Wain*: The Big Dipper.

4.548. *Nabataean waves*: Walter uses Nabataea, properly a designation for northern Arabia, as a general synonym for "the East"—despite the fact that here Alexander is himself well to the east of that region.

4.647. *Ulysses' cleverness*: "He says this because Ulysses was a faithless and treacherous man, and so Ulysses is mentioned as a model of all treacherous men." (V)

Book Five

5.1. *According to the law*: "Romulus established a ten-month year. Numa Pompilius later added two months, to wit, January and February, placing those before the rest, as Ovid attests in the first book of the *Fasti*." (V)

5.5. *with doubled shouts*: "He says this because the sun is in Gemini for fifteen days both in May and likewise in June. Thus by this he indicates that the battle took place in mid-May." (V)

5.12. *the goat had come*: "He says this since the prophets knew things to come, as though they were already past, and therefore they spoke of the future in the past tense, and so the prophet Daniel [chap. 8]: 'The goat came from the dry northern regions who would break the ram's two horns'. . . . By the goat we should understand Alexander, wanton and stinking like a goat because he was a sodomite; by the ram, Darius; by the two horns of the ram, Darius' two kingdoms, to wit, Persia and Media; by the dry northern regions we understand Europe, in which the North Wind blows, and Alexander came from Europe." (V) The allusion to Daniel's prophecy will recur in the opening of Book Six.

5.39. *Cybele*: The earth.

5.57. *the Nemean Boar*: Walter here conflates two of Hercules' labors, the slaying of the Nemean Lion and of the Erymanthian Boar.

5.92. *to pass over in silence*: "Note that once when Alexander dined with his knights, they passed to words of boasting. Clitus said, 'I have many times protected Alexander beneath my shield.' Alexander was enraged over this and charged the doorkeeper that when the knights came out he should ask each his name. Alexander himself stood hidden behind the door or gate, and when each came out, the doorkeeper asked his name. Clitus came up, and when the doorman asked him his name, he answered, 'I am Clitus the Brightest.' Upon hearing this, Alexander drew his sword and slew him." (V)

5.164. *two sisters helped the third*: Clotho and Lachesis assisted Atropos in her usual task of cutting the thread of life.

5.272. *Pallas' face and hideous arms*: Athena's aegis bore the head of Medusa, the snake-haired Gorgon slain by Perseus.

5.280. *Atlas' tireless and wind-footed scion*: Mercury.

5.350. *you fall to Scylla while you shun Charybdis*: This line was widely known in excerpt and achieved proverbial status.

5.409. *Herculean Gades*: On the Atlantic coast of Spain.

5.453. *So Lydia beheld a humbled Croesus*: "Croesus, King of Lydia, consulted Phoebus when he wished to fight against Cyrus, King of Persia, and this was the answer he received: 'Croesus will waste mighty kingdoms when he has crossed the Halys.' Phoebus meant that he would waste, that is, lose them; but Croesus understood, he would waste, that is, destroy them. And so he fought and was vanquished. One night, Croesus dreamt that Jupiter gave him water to wash his hands, but Phoebus held the towel; and he told this to his daughter. She said, 'This means you will be hanged. Jupiter, who is the upper air, will drench you with showers; but Phoebus is the sun: he will dry you; therefore do not fight further against Cyrus.' But he would not believe his daughter. He fought once again and was hanged by Cyrus." (C)

5.509. *the baked-brick walls*: As above in Book Two, Babylon is identified with the Babel of Genesis 11.

5.512. *Semiramis' town*: Queen Semiramis, wife of Ninus, King of Assyria, and legendary founder of Babylon.

5.513. *from the Seine's broad waters*: "That is, from the city of Paris, to wit, two leagues." (V)

5.548. *blooms and verdant branches*: "One finds similar events in the Gospel: 'And they cut branches from the trees and strewed his path.' So here as well, branches and flowers are strewn before Alexander in the road." (V)

5.572. *at Leucas*: "Augustus, emperor of Rome, fought against Antony near Leucas and the promontory of Actium and conquered him. In honor of his triumph, he changed the name of that month, which was then called 'Sextilis,' because it was sixth from March, but thereafter was called August, after Augustus the conqueror. But in grief at this victory Cleopatra, Antony's wife, suckled serpents at her breasts and so died wretchedly." (V)

5.576. *Emathia's battlefield*: "The battle between Caesar and Pompey took place in Emathia, which is named for 'emath,' which is blood, since there occurred a great outpouring of blood, whence Lucan's poem begins, 'Bella per Emathios,' etc." (V)

5.586. *the Spanish poet*: Lucan.

5.587. *Claudian*: A late fourth-century poet, who wrote verses in honor of the Emperor Honorius and his general.

5.594. *the True Faith would shine forth*: The anachronistc excursus into the rhetoric of the Crusades closes Book Five by bringing the reader back to the allusions to illustrious Roman deeds at the opening of Book One, and to Walter's dedicatee William of the White Hands. The "Franks" to whose king Walter here refers may denote the crusaders in Palestine (known collectively as "Franks," regardless of national origin) rather than the French.

Book Six

6.64. *Emperor Theodosius*: The reference is to Claudian's celebration of Theodosius' victory over barbarians at the edge of the Empire in the fourth century.

6.214. *ten thousand keels*: "Xerxes, desiring to cross the sea against the Greeks, was raised up in pride at his own power and said, 'I shall go through the sea dry-shod and sail upon the mountains.' And so he had a bridge of ships constructed, and thus he walked through the sea dry-shod. Later he had Mount Athos excavated, channeled the sea through the middle of the ridge, and so sailed through the mountains." (V)

6.281. *shorn of Venus' tinder*: Euctemon's metaphor may refer to physical attractiveness in general, but probably more pointedly to the castration of some of the captives.

6.562. *leader of the Grecian cohort*: "When Alexander conquered Athens, he ordered three hundred knights to be exiled. They transferred themselves to the service of Darius, and their leader was Patron, or else Timodes: and so there may have been several leaders among them, since above in the second book he said that Timodes was their leader, but here he says Patron." (V)

6.584. *enduring with the poet*: The promise that Walter's verses will confer immortality is substantially repeated of Darius at 7.381–82, and of the poem's dedicatee at 10.561–62.

6.624. *"His eye on wealth alone . . . ."*: I attribute the following lines to Bessus as direct quotation. The emphasis on exile and mercenary service accords better with Patron's circumstances than with those of Bessus himself, to whom they would apply if we take the lines as the narrator's own aside on the latter's motivation. I depart in this from the punctuation of Colker's edition, as well as from Pritchard's prose translation.

Book Seven

7.3. *Latona's virgin daughter*: Diana, the moon.

7.9. *Thetis*: a sea goddess, and mother of Achilles.

7.138. *Typhoeus*: A rebellious monster destroyed by Jupiter and buried under Mt. Etna (Ovid, *Metamorphoses* 3.303).

7.152. *the Delian*: Apollo; the sun, in other words, is at its height.

7.278. *in Indic speech*: "That is, in Chaldean. Or perhaps it could actually be in Greek, since Darius knew the Greek language, as above we have read that Patron spoke Greek with Darius, and Bessus did not understand, but rather *through interpreters. . . learned what his words had meant* [6.610–11].'" (V)

7.345. *Liber*: An archaic Roman god of agriculture, often conflated with Bacchus, but here mentioned as a separate figure, at least for elegant variation. Both are metonymies for wine.

7.347. *Simon's heirs*: "Those who sell or buy churches and monasteries are called simoniacs after Simon Magus, who wanted to buy access to the churches from the blessed Apostle Peter, that he might sell such access more dearly. He wanted, in fact, to buy the power to heal the sick by his words. Blessed Peter said to him, 'May your money go with you into perdition. Cursed be the man who sells the inheritance of God' [Acts 8:18–20]. And note that simoniacs are otherwise known as Gehazites, but they differ in that simoniacs sell and buy, while Gehazites only sell. They are so named after Gehazi, the disciple of Elisha [2 Kings 5:20–27]." (V)

7.351. *No beardless boy*: "The author says this because in his time a youth was elected bishop of Chartres on the strength of his noble lineage, though he was under thirty years old. For three things are required for episcopal ordination, to wit, the age of thirty, knowledge, and virtue." (V) This gloss is noteworthy, since it suggests that thirteenth-century readers commonly understood the condemnatory reference to be directed against Walter's dedicatee (born 1135, ordained bishop of Chartres 1164).

7.356. *who derive their name* a cardine: I.e., the cardinals, officials of the Roman church who derive their title from their "hinge" or "key" position. The etymologizing circumlocution is Walter's way of getting around the metrical unusability of the term *cardinales* (one short syllable between two longs).

7.358. *two lords over the world*: In 1159 the Holy Roman Emperor Frederick Barbarossa opposed the election of Pope Alexander III, supporting instead the antipope Victor IV, who was elected by a dissenting minority of the cardinals. The schism lasted for seventeen years; Alexander excommunicated Frederick in 1165.

7.362. *bishops, slain without respect*: The bishops in question are Thomas Becket of Canterbury (+1170) and Robert of Cambrai (+1174). It is worth noting that while a gloss in R makes this identification, glosses in both G and V assert that the reference is to Becket and to Robert, Count of Flanders, "a very just man, a bishop as it were, and so he calls him a bishop." (V)

7.420–77. The third and last of the poem's ecphrases, the description of the tomb of Darius calls to mind the legends on the oversize *mappae mundi* of the High Middle Ages, just as the ecphrasis of Apelles' earlier design in Book Four suggests the stripped-down language of the *tituli* accompanying medieval iconographic cycles. On this ecphrasis as a representation of a "T-O" map, see Christine Ratkowitsch, *Descriptio picturae: Die literarische Funktion der Beschreibung von Kunstwerken in der lateinischen Grossdichtung des 12. Jahrhunderts* (Vienna: Verlag der Österreichischen Academie der Wissenschaften, 1991), pp. 167–68. The passage was of sufficient cultural currency that Chaucer's Wife of Bath alludes to it in passing in her Prologue (ll. 503–5). The monumental world map, glossed across its surface with detailed annotations on peoples, geography, and events, has among its most celebrated examples the Hereford Map (c. 1280) and the Ebstorf Map (probably created in 1239, but known since its destruction in Hanover in 1943 from meticulous previous reproductions). See P.D.A. Harvey, *Medieval Maps* (Toronto: Unversity of Toronto Press, 1991), chap. 2. Earlier (and far smaller) examples of the genre include the so-called Henry of Mainz Map in Cambridge, Corpus Christi College MS 66. Whether Walter had in mind monumental maps that existed in his own day perhaps remains a moot point; but one might venture to speculate that the wide currency of Walter's poem might have meant that this ecphrasis itself exercized some influence on the creation of the Hereford and Ebstorf maps. As regards the use of a world description for the decoration of a tomb, one should note that the great *mappae mundi* themselves functioned as a reminder of God's universal rule and of mortality: labels at the edges of the Hereford Map bear the letters M, O, R, and S, thus spelling out DEATH, while on the Ebstorf Map, Christ's head, hands, and feet project beyond the edges of the world. See Maura K. Lafferty, "Mapping Human Limitations: The Tomb Ecphrases in Walter of Châtillon's *Alexandreis*," *Journal of Medieval Latin* 4 (1994), 64–81; see also the note on 1.459 above. Walter's notably anachronistic descriptions of peoples and lands also suggest the panoptic vision of the world seen *sub specie aeternitatis*; but less sublimely, they raise the question of the pleasure thirteenth-century readers may have felt in their own perceptions of such incongruities. Such anachronisms are in any case characteristic of surviving medieval world maps as well.

7.431. *four equisdistant columns*: The materials as described here by Walter might well suggest the prophecy in Daniel 2, in which a statue with gold head, silver breast, bronze belly and thighs, legs of iron, and feet of clay symbolizes the succession of kingdoms.

7.439. *the tripart world*: The threefold division of the common "T-O" schema explained above in the note on 1.459.

7.476. *The sum of years*: Walter on several occasions uses elaborate distributive combinations as circumlocutions for compound numbers. In general, I translate these in simplified form, but here I provide a more literal rendition, since the numerology clearly contributes to the prophetic tone of the monument and its inscriptions.

Book Eight

8.7. *the supplications of the lisping Bagoas*: "Here he says that Narbazanes was reconciled to Alexander by pretty words, but the author is reticent about the truth, that Narbazanes had two very beautiful sons whom Alexander abused. They begged peace from Alexander on behalf of their father Narbazanes; but since this redounds to Alexander's dishonor, the author therefore keeps quiet." (V)

8.9. *Talestris of the Amazons*: Walter adheres closely to Curtius' account of the encounter between Alexander and the visiting queen but departs in telling details from his prose source. The account of the face-to-face meeting and of Talestris' proposition differs in substance from another well-known version of the encounter between them in the *Historia de preliis*, where communication goes on through a series of letters. For a close reading of the passage, see David Townsend, "Sex and the Single Amazon in Twelfth-Century Latin Epic," *University of Toronto Quarterly* 64 (1995), 255–73.

8.59. *exchanging his old name*: "Either because he was earlier called a servant, but now a lord, or else because he ordered that as king he be called Oxatreus, which was the name of Darius' brother." (V)

8.85–388. The trial of Philotas is the longest single episode in the *Alexandreis*. Book Eight thus forms something of a diptych, of which the second half is the speech of the Scythian messenger in lines 434–557, with its frank indictment of Alexander's hubris. The two passages are prefaced by Talestris' appearance, hinged by meditations on the fall of Philotas and of Bessus, and closed off by the narrator's brief observation that Alexander disregarded the Scythian messenger and conquered the land despite his exhortations. The trial and the account of the plot of which Philotas stands accused is much telescoped from the lengthy version in Book 6 of Curtius. "In evidence of those matters spoken of here, it must be observed how this conspiracy arose. Demetrius, Dimus, and Lecolaus indeed conspired toward Alexander's death. One day, while Dimus was in the temple of Athena, he sighed deeply, and Nicomachus asked why. He answered, 'I and some others have conspired against Alexander.' Having heard this, Nicomachus told everything to Cebalinus, and Cebalinus reported it to Philotas. Philotas kept silent about the disclosure for three days, perhaps because he thought the report was false, perhaps because he had no opportunity to speak with Alexander. At last the rumor reached Metron, the king's praetor, who kept silent about the treachery not even for an hour. And since Philotas had kept silent, he was accused as chief of the conspiracy." (V)

8.195. *the rightful penalty of regicide*: "Burchard was the murderer of Count Robert of Flanders. Louis, King of France, had him killed by breaking his limbs on a wheel of torture with nails fastened to it." (V) (These events took place under Louis VI in 1127.)

8.264. *the theft of Pallas' image*: For the contest of Ajax and Odysseus for the armor of Achilles, see Ovid, *Metamorphoses*, Book 13.

8.408. *the Stygian sisters*: the Furies.

8.410. *while Bessus strove to rise*: The moralization on Bessus' fate parallels that on Philotas' immediately preceding, and both exemplify the Wheel of Fortune topos ubiquitous in medieval literature.

8.416. *the Tanais*: The Iaxartes.

Book Nine

9.6. *that teacher second only to great Aristotle*: Callisthenes, Aristotle's nephew, who accompanied Alexander's expedition as chronicler but who was executed for alleged complicity in the assasination plot.

9.7–8. *a clear lesson to coming generations*: V provides a gloss on Clitus more or less repeating that translated in the note on 5.92 above and then continues: "Hermolaus was a youth who hunted with Alexander in a forest. A stag ran before him, and he killed it, and Alexander was consequently enraged, because he had not left the stag for him to kill instead. He struck Hermolaus, so that Hermolaus wept. Seeing this, Callisthenes rebuked him and said, 'Remember that you are a man,' as if he were saying, 'Stop weeping, since you are a man,' but Alexander took it adversely, to wit, 'Remember that you are a man,' or in other words, 'Avenge yourself, since you are a man.' And so Alexander had them both killed."

9.22. *the Red Sea*: Medieval cartography often made no distinction among the Red Sea, the Gulf of Persia, and the northwestern Indian Ocean.

9.27. *the Achesis*: Classically, the Acesines, i.e., the Chenab.

9.84–164. The episode of Nicanor and Symachus is closely modeled on the doomed expedition of Nisus and Euryalus in *Aeneid* 9.

9.241–42. *Rubricus now rubricated earth*: The word play reproduces that in the original. Paranomasia on proper names figures largely in twelfth- and thirteenth-century Latin poetry, often in contexts where the puns may strike a modern reader as inappropriate to moments of high seriousness. It is worth remembering in such contexts what authority the practice drew from the tradition of Isidore's widely read sixth-century encyclopedia, the *Etymologiae*.

9.308. *Pellaeus named a city in his honor*: "Which the Alexandrians call Bucephala. Every year Alexander founded a city, whence Ovid says, 'He founded in twelve years twelve cities' walls, which seemly honor of his name adorned.'" (C) (The quotation is in fact drawn from the *Aurora* of Peter Riga.)

9.337. *with the peoples of Avernus*: With the shades of the Underworld.

9.662. *the shores of the Antipodes*: Those familiar with the cosmography of Dante will recognize immediately the geographical assumptions operating here. Some T-O maps provide space beyond the encircling Ocean for a fourth continent, the Antipodes. There, opposite the center of the known world (Jerusalem), lay the earthly paradise of Eden. Alexander's project thus involves a level of hubris that makes the Goddess Nature's impending retaliation in Book Ten all the more readily intelligible.

Book Ten

10.6. *Nature with a mindful grief*: The personification of Nature as a goddess mediating between the creative agency of the Christian God and the world of matter reflects the syncretic Neoplatonism of a substantial body of thought in twelfth-century northern France: see also the note on 4.229 above. Among her other principal literary appearances in the twelfth century are the *Cosmographia* of Bernardus Silvestris and the *De planctu naturae* of Alan of Lille.

10.110. *and lay siege to Paradise*: See the note on 9.662 above.

10.154. *Still is that fated*: The prophecy, of course, refers properly to Christ's Harrowing of Hell between Good Friday and Easter morning. Satan here is no better an interpreter of phatic utterance than Alexander proved to be of the words of the Hebrew High Priest in Book One.

10.192. *carried through Sicilian skies*: Mt. Etna and other locations in Sicily were considered entrances to the Underworld.

10.489–90. *those brothers buried at Etna*: See the note on 7.138 above.

10.531. *the walls of greedy Rome*: Invective against the Roman Curia and its vices, notably its greed, is a staple of twelfth-century satirical verse, including Walter's own rhythmical poems.

10.550. *another fount*: "That is, God, the living fountain of all goodness, of whom the Gospel says, 'I am the living fountain; he who drinks from me shall not thirst again [John 4:13–14].'" (V)

Index of Proper Names

This index does not cover references to the most ubiquitous proper names, including Alexander, Asia, Darius, Europe, Greece, Macedonia, Persia, and Porus. Personifications of abstract qualities are also omitted, except where they figure significantly as characters. Here and in the translation, the spelling of most names is adjusted from that of the Latin text to accord with the expectations of anglophone readers: English conventions, for both classical and biblical names, override the spellings of the Vulgate Latin and, where necessary, of classical norms, but classical norms generally override medieval respellings: thus "Ptolemy" rather than classical Latin "Ptolomaeus" or medieval "Tolomeus"; "Euphrates" rather than "Eufrates"; "Mazaeus" rather than "Mazeus"; "Elijah" rather than "Elias." In a few cases I have preserved the Latin text's substantive phonetic modification of classical forms, generally in the names of minor characters in the Alexander tradition.

www.ingramcontent.com/pod-product-compliance
Lightning Source LLC
Chambersburg PA
CBHW070632310726
48982CB00001B/259

* 9 7 8 0 8 1 2 2 3 3 4 7 6 *